# Have You Spiritually Been Born of God?

# Have You Spiritually Been Born of God?

## Quotes by Ancient and Latter-day Prophets and Apostles

Compiled by Sarah F. Smith

Printed in the United States of America
by DesignPubGroup.com

# Contents

# Introduction

This book is a collection of quotes from both ancient and modern prophets and apostles on the subject of being spiritually born of God, born again, spiritual rebirth, the baptism of fire, the gift of the Holy Ghost as a constant companion, conversion, sanctification, purification, the mighty change of heart, and becoming His sons and daughters. I have also included some of my own thoughts, which I hope will be enlightening to you. Of course, the words I have written are according to my own understanding, and are <u>not</u> official doctrine or statements by the Church of Jesus Christ of Latter-day Saints.

My only desire in compiling these quotes, is to help build up the kingdom of God on the earth. By myself, I am weak, and can not write even one inspired word on my own. However, with the Lord's help "all things are possible to him who believeth." I have prayed continually that the words I write will be according to His will. Over the past several years, I have felt prompted and encouraged by the Spirit to compile this book, and I will be forever grateful to the Lord, for the handful of very choice friends He has placed in my life; valiant souls, who truly understand what it means to be spiritually born of God. Their understanding is not only in their minds, but also in their hearts. These dear friends have been very supportive to me, and to this endeavor.

I have chosen to not list my credentials, because I believe this practice places one person above another, this encourages pride, and increases the distance between people. I prefer speaking to you as a dear friend, a person of infinite worth, with whom I can share the deep feelings of my heart.

We probably have many things in common. I was raised in the Church of

Jesus Christ of Latter-day Saints and, when I was about 13 years old, I had a strong desire to know of the truthfulness of the gospel for myself. The Lord blessed me with a strong testimony, which has continually grown. Later, I was privileged to attend BYU and enjoyed the spiritual atmosphere there. I met a choice companion, and we were married in the temple. We have been blessed with wonderful children, and beautiful grandchildren. Over the years, we have served the Lord in a variety of church callings.

I love my Savior, Jesus Christ, with all my heart, and He has greatly blessed me through the many trials that have come into my life. His divine hands have always been outstretched, patiently waiting for me to open the door to my heart and let Him in.

For years, I trudged along, believing that I needed to be spiritually self-reliant. I have always remained totally active in the Church, and my testimony has never wavered. However, my belief in spiritual self-reliance kept me from truly coming to my Lord and Redeemer. It wasn't until the heavy burdens in my life weighed me down intensely and I was at the breaking point (both physically and emotionally), that I finally came to the Savior with a broken heart and a contrite spirit. Finally, I turned my life over to Him, and He has turned my life of sorrow, pain and stress, into one of great joy, love and peace. I will be forever grateful for the marvelous blessings he has, and continues, to pour out upon me.

I know that the Lord also loves you with a perfect and very personal love. **Jesus, and our Heavenly Parents, love you so intensely, it is as if you were their only child**. Let these words penetrate into your heart, pray with sincerity to have a witness of their truthfulness, keep the commandments and you will feel God's deep personal love for you grow in intensity.

If you have had the privilege of becoming a parent, may I invite you to think back to when you held your newborn baby in your arms? Remember the intense love you felt for your child. As loving parents, we love each child as much as if that child were our only one. However, our love is imperfect and we do not know all of our children's thoughts and feelings as intimately as our Heavenly Parents know us.

In comparison, imagine your Heavenly Parents, and your Savior's perfect love. They know all of your thoughts, feelings and the intents of your heart. (Alma 18:32) They know you better than you know yourself. For thousands, and perhaps millions of years, you were nurtured continually with celestial love. You are a Child of God, a potential god, and you really are loved, so personally that it is as if, you were their only child. They cherish you, and each of us, with an everlasting love which surpasses our understanding. Certainly, they want us to not only say "I am a Child of God", but to feel it! To feel it with every fiber of our souls and to be filled with faith, hope, love, truth and exceeding great joy!

This type of joy is poured upon all who are spiritually born of God. This exceeding great joy was given to King Benjamin's people. In Mosiah 4:20 we read, *"he has poured out his Spirit upon you, and has caused that your hearts should be filled with joy, and has caused that your mouths should be stopped that ye could not find utterance, so exceedingly great was your joy."* To be filled with this great joy we must come unto Him. For Jesus said, *"Draw near unto me and I will draw near unto you; seek me diligently and ye shall find me; ask, and ye shall receive; knock, and it shall be opened unto you."* (D&C 88:63)

It is my prayer that these words of the prophets and apostles, who are quoted in this book, will sink deep into your heart. So that you may be taught by the Spirit, that your mind and heart may be freed from self-justifications, rationalizations, misunderstandings, and pride. It is also my prayer that the Spirit of humility, meekness, wisdom, faith, hope, and love to be poured into your heart as you study, ponder and pray to have a witness of the truth. I hope that you will really listen to the literalness of each quote, and remember that the Lord delights in plainness. (D&C 133:57)

However, I feel impressed by the Spirit to warn you, because the Lord has said, *"For of him unto whom much is given much is required; and he who sins against the greater light shall receive the greater condemnation"* (D&C 82:3) If you are reading this book because you love truth, and you want to know your standing before the Lord, and you are willing to "do" whatever He requires of you, then drink deeply of these words of the prophets.

On the other hand, if you are reading this book with the belief that you already know everything there is to be learned about spiritual rebirth; if you are unwilling to be totally honest in your self-introspection; if you are unwilling to strive to "live by every word that proceedeth forth from the mouth of God" (D&C 84:44) then is may NOT be the right time for you to learn these things. For you will be held accountable for what you have learned, but have refused to do. There is much given in these quotes from the prophets and much is required. And if you sin against the greater light you shall receive a greater condemnation.

Please set this book down right now and pray to know if it is God's will for you to receive these things at this time in your life. It is my hope that you will pray with faith, with real intent, with all the sincerity of your heart, that you may know the Lord's will, before you continue reading.

May the Lord's choicest blessings be given to you, according to His will, and may you "hunger and thirst after righteousness," that you may "be filled with the Holy Ghost" (3 Nephi 12:6), and "with exceeding great joy." (Alma 4:14)

**Author's Note:**
*I have highlighted many words throughout the text to encourage you to emphasize these phrases, which may open a deeper understanding to familiar scriptures.*

# CHAPTER 1

# *"Study it out in Your Mind"*

Have you spiritually been born of God? Perhaps this question is one of the most important inquires we can take to the Lord, in order to discover our standing with Him. How does one really know if he has been spiritually born of God? *"If any of you lack wisdom, let him ask of God, that giveth to all men liberally, and upbraideth not; and it shall be given him. But let him ask in faith, nothing wavering…"* (James 1:5, 6)

In your quest to really know if you have been born of God. It is important to thoroughly understand the doctrine, by studying the scriptures that have reference to this marvelous change of heart. Remember the Lord's council to Oliver Cowdery in the Doctrine & Covenants 9:7-8, *"Behold, you have not understood; you supposed that I would give it unto you, when you took no thought save it was to ask me. But, behold I say unto you, that you must study it out in your mind; then you must ask me it be right, and if it is right I will cause that your bosom shall burn within you; there fore, you shall feel that it is right."*

The great prophet Moroni also instructs us to first read and ponder the truth before we ask God. In Moroni 10:3-5 he states, *"Behold, I would exhort you that when ye shall read these things, **if it be wisdom in God that ye should read them**, that ye would remember how merciful the Lord hath been unto the children of men, from the creation of Adam even down until the time that ye shall receive these things, I would exhort you that ye would ask God, the Eternal Father in the name of Christ, if these things are not true; and if ye shall ask with a sincere heart, with real intent, having faith in Christ, he will* *manifest the truth of it unto you, by the power of the Holy Ghost. And by the power of the Holy Ghost ye may know the truth of all things."* Thus, you can know if you have been spiritually born of God.

As you study this sacred subject, I would like to invite you to sincerely pray each time you begin reading, remembering to ask Heavenly Father to bless you with the Spirit, that you may *"...seek learning by study and also by faith"* (D&C 88:118). The Lord reminds us to *"Ask, and ye shall receive; knock, and it shall be opened unto you."* (D&C 4:7) Certainly the Spirit is more likely to open our minds and touch our hearts, when we pray for it to be with us. Jesus tells us that when *"...the Spirit of truth, is come, he will guide you into all truth..."* (John 16:13) and again He says in D&C 75:10, *"Calling on the name of the Lord for the Comforter, which shall teach them all things that are expedient for them."*

As you study, remember the Lord delights in plainness. He means exactly what he says, *"for I would be plain unto you according to the plainness of truth"* (2 Nephi 9:47). *"And now, my brethren, I have spoken plainly that ye cannot err."* (2 Nephi 25:20) *"...for the Spirit speaketh the truth and lieth not. Wherefore, it speaketh of things as they really are and of things as they really will be; wherefore these things are manifested unto us plainly, for the salvation of our souls. But behold, we are not witnesses alone in these things; for God also spake them unto prophets of old."* (Jacob 4:13)

In the Doctrine and Covenants 93:31 the Lord said, *"...because that which was from the beginning is plainly manifest unto them, and they receive not the light."* In D&C 133:57-58 we read, *"...that men might be made partakers of the glories which were to be revealed, the Lord sent forth the fulness of his gospel, his everlasting covenant, reasoning in plainness and simplicity-To prepare the weak for those things which are coming on the earth, and for the Lord's errand in the day when the weak shall confound the wise..."*

When we accept the scriptures in their plainness, simplicity, and literalness we are also accepting the true celestial definition of His words, instead of the telestial watered down, half truth interpretations which often ensnares one into "justifying himself." (Luke 10:29) When a man seeketh to justify himself, he is not being lead by the Spirit, for "it is God that justifieth." (Romans 8:33)

I hope that you will read these quotes and scriptures, as if you are reading them for the first time, so your mind will be open to the promptings of the Spirit. For can anyone be taught by the Spirit, if he believes he already knows everything on the subject? Without true humility, and a teachable disposition, one may study the gospel for years, and be *ever learning, and never able to come to a knowledge of the truth.*" (2 Timothy 3:7).

In a concluding paragraph of Elder Bruce R. McConkie's book "Doctrine and Covenants Commentary" p. 863 he wrote the following, *"Reading is not sufficient. We must KEEP THE REVELATIONS in our memories and meditate upon them; we must keep them in our affection, so that we **love them, as we would a message from our dearest friends;** we must put their **teachings into practice.** If we are weary and exhausted, hungry and thirsty, it is no satisfaction to sit down to a table laden with food and pure water, and to admire the things provided; we must partake thereof, until our wants are supplied, and we must do so every day. It is the same with the spiritual nourishment. We must make it part of ourselves by **putting into practice the truths revealed.**"*

To receive spiritual nourishment, humbly ask the Lord for further light and knowledge and then in gratitude, strive *"to live by every word which proceedeth from the mouth of God."*(D&C 84:44) Those who are truly humble and teachable are willing to change their lives, and put into practice the truths they have been given.

In D&C 136:32-33 we read, *"Let him that is ignorant* (we are all ignorant in many things) *learn wisdom by **humbling** himself and calling upon the Lord his God, that his eyes may be opened that he may see, and his ears opened that he may hear; for my Spirit is sent forth into the world to **enlighten the humble** and contrite, and to the condemnation of the ungodly."*

The ungodly are also the proud who disregard the true meaning of the scriptures, *"But behold, there are many that harden their hearts against the Holy Spirit, that it hath no place in them; wherefore, they cast many things away which are written and esteem them as things of naught."*(2 Nephi 33:2) In Alma 12:10-11, the Lord also tells us, *"And therefore, he that will harden his heart, the same receiveth the lesser portion of the word; and he that will **not harden his heart, to him is given the greater portion of the word,** until it is given unto him to know the mysteries of God until he knows them in full. And they that will harden their hearts, to them is given the lesser portion of the word until they know nothing concerning his mysteries; and they are taken captive by the devil, and led by his will down to destruction. Now this is what is meant by the chains of hell."*

Therefore, humility is an essential attribute we need to possess so that we will be ready to be taught by the Holy Spirit. The Lord tells us in *D&C 112:10,* *"**Be thou humble; and the Lord thy God shall lead thee by the hand, and give thee answer to thy prayers.**"*

Pres. Joseph F. Smith said, *"If I have learned something through prayer, supplication, and **perseverance** in **seeking** to know the truth, and I tell it to you, it will not be knowledge unto you. I can tell you how you can obtain it, **but I cannot give it to you. If we receive this knowledge, it must come from the Lord. He can touch your understandings and your spirits, so that you shall comprehend perfectly and not be mistaken. But I cannot do that. You can obtain this knowledge through repentance, humility, and seeking the Lord with full purpose of heart until you find Him. He is not afar off. It is not difficult to approach Him, if we will only do it with a broken heart and a contrite spirit, as did Nephi of old.**"* (CR, Oct. 1899, p.71)

It is my hope that you will press forward, feasting upon the words of Christ, with an open mind and heart, so that you may more clearly understand the fullness of His gospel. May the Spirit of humility, repentance, faith and love be with you while you journey on your quest to come closer to Christ, and to know if you have been spiritually born of God.

# CHAPTER 2

# "Filled with Exceeding Great Joy"

What does it mean to be "filled with exceeding great joy"? Is it more than a wonderful testimony building experience? Is being filled with this great spiritual joy *felt* by those who are spiritually born of God? Is this intense joy a witness to ones soul that the "mighty change of heart" has truly come to pass?

The Book of Mormon has several priceless accounts of those who were filled with exceeding great joy. In the book of Enos verse 3-6, the prophet Enos said, *"the words which I had often heard my father speak concerning* **eternal life***, and the* **joy of the saints***, sunk deep into my heart. And my* **soul hungered;***"* Could it be that Enos hungered for the exceeding great joy which is spoken of many times in the scriptures, and is associated with receiving a remission of ones sins?

Isn't it reasonable to assume that Enos already had a strong testimony and had always tried to keep the commandments? Especially, since he was influenced daily by his father, the prophet Jacob, and by his uncle, the prophet Nephi. Obviously, they had thoroughly taught him the holy scriptures from a young age.

Enos realized that he had sometimes fallen short. He had sinned and transgressed God's commandments, just as we all have, at times. Enos also knew that in order to receive the marvelous gift, of being "filled with the Holy Spirit" and "exceeding great joy" that he needed to confess **all** of his sins and transgressions to God, with a broken heart, and a contrite spirit.

"*And my soul hungered; and I kneeled down before my Maker, and I **cried** unto him in **mighty prayer** and supplication for mine own soul; and all the day long did I cry unto him; yea, and when the night came I did still raise my voice high that it reached the heavens. And there came a voice unto me saying; Enos, **thy sins are forgiven thee**, and thou shalt be blessed. And I, Enos, knew that God could not lie; wherefore, **my guilt was swept away.**"* (Enos 4) Certainly, Enos' soul was filled with great joy when he knew that all of his sins were totally forgiven.

Another wonderful example of those who were filled with exceeding great joy are King Benjamin's people. They were the faithful members of the church, who came to hear the inspired words of their beloved Prophet. They listened with the Spirit, and were taught how to come to the Lord with a broken heart, that they may be spiritually born of God and receive all of the great blessings that the mighty change of heart brings.

In Mosiah 4:2-3 we read, "*And they had viewed themselves in their own carnal state, even less than the dust of the earth. And they all cried aloud with one voice, saying: O have mercy, and apply the atoning blood of Christ that we may receive **forgiveness** of our sins, and our **hearts may be purified;** for we believe in Jesus Christ, the Son of God, who created heaven and earth, and all things; who shall come down among the children of men. And it came to pass that after they had spoken these words the Spirit of the Lord came upon them, and they were **filled with joy,** having received a **remission of their sins**, and having **peace of conscience** because of the **exceeding faith** which they had in Jesus Christ who should come, according to the words which king Benjamin had spoken unto them.*"

As chapter 4 continues, we learn more about being filled with exceeding great joy. In Mosiah 4:11-12, 20, "*...as ye have come to the knowledge of the glory of God, or if ye have known of his goodness and have **tasted of his love,** and have **received a remission of your sins, which causeth such exceedingly great joy in your souls,** even so I would that ye should remember, and always retain in **remembrance**, the greatness of God...and **humble** yourselves even in the depths of humility, **calling** on the name of the Lord daily, and standing* *steadfastly in the **faith** of that which is to come, which was spoken by the mouth of the angel. And behold, I say unto you that if ye do this ye shall always rejoice, and be **filled with the love of God,** and always **retain a remission of your sins;** and ye shall **grow in the knowledge** of the **glory of him** that created you, or in the knowledge of that which is just and true.".…"And behold, even at this time, ye have been calling on his name, and **begging** for a **remission of your sins**. And has he suffered that ye have begged in vain? Nay; he has poured out his Spirit upon you, and has caused that your hearts should be **filled with joy,** and has caused that your mouths should be stopped that ye **could not find utterance,** so **exceedingly great was your joy.**"*

These faithful members of the church followed the process of coming to the Lord with a totally broken, repentant heart. This marvelous blessing was poured out upon the multitude, teaching us that becoming spiritually born of God is a miraculous event, which is proceeded by the process of developing sufficient faith, and repentance. Then this great blessing is given to all whom the Spirit will justify. For most, becoming spiritually ready to be born of God is a process which usually requires an extended length of time. However, being born of God is an actual event. There are many personal testimonies and scriptures that support this truth.

The following was written by Pres. Lorenzo Snow, *"When receiving the baptism of the Holy Ghost I know I was immersed in a divine principle that filled my whole system with **inexpressible joy;** and from that day to the present have blessings crowned my labors. And when baptizing people and administering the ordinances of this holy priesthood, God has confirmed those administrations by imparting the Holy Ghost, giving a knowledge to the individuals to whom I administered, convincing them that the authority was delegated from heaven."* LDPDC, Vol 2, p 207

Pres. Lorenzo Snow also wrote, *"I was baptized by Elder John Boynton, then one of the Twelve Apostles, June, 1836, at Kirtland, Ohio. Previous to accepting the ordinance of baptism, in my investigations of the principles taught by the Latter-day Saints, which I proved by comparison to be the same as those mentioned in the New Testament taught by Christ and His Apostles, I was thoroughly convinced that obedience to those principles would impart miraculous powers, manifestations and revelations. With expectation of this result, I received baptism and the ordinance of laying on of hands by one who professed to have divine authority; and having thus yielded obedience to these ordinances, I was in constant expectation of the fulfillment of the promise of the reception of the Holy Ghost. The* **manifestation did not immediately follow my baptism** *as I had expected, but although the time was deferred, when I did receive it,* **its realization was more perfect, tangible and miraculous than even my strongest hopes** *had led me to anticipate.*

*Some two or three weeks after I was baptized, one day while engaged in my studies, I began to reflect upon the fact that I had not obtained a knowledge of the truth of the work-that I had not realized the fulfillment of the promise, 'he that doeth my will shall know of the doctrine,' and I began to feel very uneasy. I laid aside my books, left the house and wondered around through the fields under the oppressive influence of a gloomy, disconsolate spirit, while an indescribable cloud of darkness seemed to envelope me. I had been accustomed, at the close of day, to retire for secret prayer, to a grove a short distance from my lodgings, but at this time I felt no inclination to do so. The spirit of prayer had departed and the heavens seemed like brass over my head., At length, realizing that the usual time had come for secret prayer, I concluded I would not fore go my evening service, and as a matter of formality, knelt as I was in the habit of doing, and in my accustomed, retired place, but not feeling as I was wont to feel. I had no sooner opened my lips in an effort to pray, than I heard a sound, just above my head, like the rustling of silken robes; and immediately the spirit of God descended upon me; completely enveloping my whole person,* **filling me** *from the crown of my head to the souls of my feet, and* **O the joy and happiness I felt. No language can describe** *the almost instantaneous transition from a dense cloud of mental and spiritual darkness into a* **refulgence of light** *and* **knowledge,** *that God lives, that Jesus Christ is the Son of God, and of the restoration of the Holy Priesthood, and the fullness of the Gospel. It was a* **complete baptism, a tangible immersion in the heavenly principle or element, the Holy Ghost;** *and even* **more real and physical in its effects upon every part of my system** *than the immersion by water;* **dispelling forever,** *so long as reason and memory last, all possibility of* **doubt or fear** *in relation to the fact* *handed down to us historically that the babe of Bethlehem is **truly the son of God**; also the fact that He is now being revealed to the children of men, and communicating knowledge, the same as in Apostolic times. I was **perfectly satisfied**, as well I might be, for my expectations were more than realized; I think I may safely say, in an infinite degree. I cannot tell how long I remained in the full flow of the **blissful enjoyment** and **divine enlightenment**, but it was several minutes before the celestial element which filled and surrounded me began gradually to withdraw. On arising from my kneeling posture, with **my heart swelling with gratitude to God,** beyond the power of expression, I felt, I knew that He had conferred on me what only an omnipotent being can confer, that which is of **greater value than all the wealth and honors** worlds can bestow. That night as I retired to rest, the same wonderful manifestations were repeated, and continued to be for several successive nights. The sweet remembrance of those glorious experiences, from that time to the present, brings them fresh before me, imparting an **inspiring influence** which **pervades my whole being**, and I trust will to the close of my earthly existence."* Deseret Book 1945 "The Presidents of the Church" by Preston Nibley

Elder Heber C. Kimball described his baptism of fire, in the following words, *"Under the ordinances of the baptism and the laying on of hands, I received the Holy Ghost, as the disciples did in ancient days, which was **like a consuming fire. I felt as though I sat at the feet of Jesus,** and was clothed in my right mind, although the people called me crazy. I continued in this way for many months, and it seemed as though my body would consume away; at the same time the **scriptures were unfolded** to my mind in such a wonderful manner that it appeared to me, at times, as if I had formerly been familiar with them."* "The Life of Heber C. Kimball" by Orson F. Whitney, Bookcraft, 1943

President Joseph F. Smith said, *"...the influence and power of the Holy Spirit that I experienced when I had been baptized for the remission of my sins. The **feeling that came upon me was that of pure peace, of love and of light.** I felt in my soul that if I had sinned-and surely I was not without sin-that it had been forgiven me; that I was **indeed cleansed from sin;** my heart was touched, and I felt that I would not injure the smallest insect beneath my feet. I felt as though I **wanted to do good everywhere** to everybody and to everything. I felt* *a newness of life, a newness of desire* to do that which was right. **There was not one particle of desire for evil left in my soul.**" (CR, April 1898 P 66, LDPDC Vol 2, p 381)

Let us return to the Book of Mormon, in Alma 19:6 we learn that King Lamoni received the light of everlasting life, *"Now, this was what Ammon desired, for he knew that king Lamoni was under the power of God; he knew that the dark veil of* **unbelief was being cast away from his mind**, *and the* **light which did light up his mind**, *which was the light of the glory of God, which was a marvelous light of his goodness-yea, this light had* **infused such joy** *into his soul, the cloud of darkness having been dispelled, and that the* **light of everlasting life was lit up in his soul**, *yea, he knew that this had* **overcome his natural frame**, *and he was carried away in God."*

Later in Alma 22, Aaron teaches King Lamoni's father, the plan of redemption. In verses 15-18 it reads, *"And it came to pass that after Aaron had expounded these things unto him, the king said: What shall I do that I may have this eternal life of which thou hast spoken? Yea, what shall I do that I may be* **born of God,** *having this* **wicked spirit rooted out of my breast**, *and* **receive his Spirit**, *that I may be* **filled with joy,** *that I may not be cast off at the last day? Behold, said he, I will give up all that I possess, yea, I will forsake my kingdom, that I may receive this* **great joy.** *But Aaron said unto him: If thou desirest this thing, if thou wilt* **bow down before God**, *yea, if thou wilt* **repent of all thy sins**, *and will bow down before God, and call on* **his name in faith, believing that ye shall receive,** *then shalt thou* **receive the hope** *which thou desirest. And it came to pass that when Aaron had said these words, the king did bow down before the Lord upon his knees; yea, even he did prostrate himself upon the earth, and* **cried mightily,** *saying: O God, Aaron hath told me that there is a God; and if there is a God, and if thou art God, wilt thou make thyself known unto me, and* **I will give away all my sins to know thee**, *and that I may be raised from the dead, and* **be saved** *at the last day."*

Are you ready to give away all of your sins, all contention, all pride, all anger, all selfishness, all self-justifying negative thinking and self-pity (which is a form of self-centeredness)? Are you ready to give up all addictions; including the TV, computer games, *the internet,* excessive eating, excessive shopping, or anything you do compulsively, in order that you may know Christ, and experience a mighty change of heart, and be filled with this exceeding great joy?

This exquisite joy is also beautifully described by Alma the younger in Alma 36: 18-26, *"Now, as my mind caught hold upon this thought, I cried within my heart: O Jesus, thou Son of God, have mercy on me, who am in the gall of bitterness, and am encircled about by the everlasting chains of death. And now, behold, when I thought this, I could remember my pains no more; yea, I was harrowed up by the memory of by sins no more. And* **oh, what joy,** *and what* **marvelous light** *I did behold; yea, my soul was* **filled with joy as exceeding as was my pain***! Yea, I say unto you, my son, that there could be nothing so exquisite and so bitter as were my pains. Yea, and again I say unto you, my son, that on the other hand, there can be* **nothing so exquisite and sweet as was my joy.** *Yea, me thought I saw, even as our father Lehi saw, God sitting upon his throne, surrounded with numberless concourses of angels, in the attitude of singing and praising their God; yea, and my soul did long to be there. But behold, my limbs did receive their strength again, and I stood upon my feet, and did manifest unto the people that I had been* **born of God.** *Yea, and from that time even until now, I have labored without ceasing, that I might bring souls unto* **repentance***; that I might bring them to taste of the* **exceeding joy** *of which I did taste; that they might also be* **born of God,** *and be* **filled with the Holy Ghost.** *Yea, and now behold, O my son, the Lord doth give me exceedingly great joy in the fruit of my labors; For because of the word which he has imparted unto me, behold,* **many have been born of God,** *and have tasted as I have tasted, and have seen eye to eye as I have seen; therefore they do know of these things of which I have spoken, as I do know; and the knowledge which I have is of God."*

Many of the people Alma taught experienced what he had experienced. They were filled with exquisite joy and they **knew** they had been born again, just as Alma knew it and testified of it. This account reaffirms the importance of being spiritually reborn, and that it isn't just the apostles and prophets, who receive this wonderful blessing.

In the New Testament, Peter writes of the unspeakable joy, the saints experienced. In Peter 1:7-10 it reads, *"That the trial of your faith, being much more precious than of gold that perisheth, though it be **tried with fire,** might be found unto praise and honor and glory at the appearing of Jesus Christ: Whom having not seen, ye love; in whom, though now ye see him not, yet believing, ye rejoice with **joy unspeakable and full of glory: Receiving the end of your faith,** even the **salvation of your souls.** Of which salvation the prophets have enquired and searched diligently, who prophesied of the grace that should come unto you:"*

Brigham Young said, *"Now compare the greatest of earthly joys with the joys you receive in believing in Jesus Christ and obeying the Gospel he has delivered to the children of men. It is sweeter than the honeycomb; and to those who live according to it, **it gives constant joy,** a lasting feast not merely for an hour or a day, but for a whole life and through out eternity. The appetite is always keen, there is always plenty for it to feast upon. This is my experience. The revelations of the Lord Jesus Christ are sweeter than honey or the honeycomb."* JD 8:139

Pres. Young also said, *"It is the province, and duty of the Latter-day Saints to **cultivate that spirit until it becomes as a living fire within them.**"* CR Apr 1899 p. 50

May your soul hunger for the mighty change of heart and the exceeding great joy, which is given to those who are spiritually born of God. May this righteous desire grow in your heart, that you may thirst for the living water, which will satisfy your soul. Because *"whosoever drinketh of the water that I shall give him shall **never thirst;** but the water that I shall give him shall be in him a well of water springing up into **everlasting life."** John 4:14 "And blessed are all they who do hunger and thirst after righteousness, for they shall be **filled with the Holy Ghost."** 3 Nephi 12:6

# CHAPTER 3

# "*They shall be Converted, and I Will Heal Them*"

Is there a difference between having a testimony and truly being converted? What did Jesus, mean when he said to Peter, ***"When thou art converted, strengthen thy brethren" Luke 22:32?*** Why did the Lord make a similar plea to the Quorum of the Twelve Apostles in D&C 112:12-13? When He said, "*And pray for thy brethren of the Twelve; Admonish them sharply for my name's sake, and let them be admonished for all their sins, and be ye faithful before me unto my name. And after their temptations, and much tribulation, behold, I the Lord, will feel after them, and if they harden not their hearts, and stiffen not their necks against me,* **they shall be converted, and I will heal them.**"

Pres. Marion G. Romney gave a conference address on this subject in Oct. 1963, where he said, "*While conversion may be accomplished in stages,* **one is not really converted in the full sense of the term unless and until he is at heart a new person. Born again is the scriptural term.**" He continues by quoting from Luke 22:31-32, "*Simon, Simon, behold Satan hath desired to have you, that he may sift you as wheat: But I have prayed for thee, that thy faith fail not: and* **when** *thou art converted, strengthen thy brethren*" *From this it would appear that* **membership in the Church and conversion are not necessarily synonymous. Being converted, as we are here using the term, and having a testimony are not necessarily the same thing either.** *A testimony comes when the Holy Ghost gives the earnest seeker a witness of the truth. A moving testimony vitalizes faith-that is, it induces repentance and obedience* to the commandments. **Conversion, on the other hand, is the fruit of, or the reward for, repentance and obedience.** *(Of course, one's testimony continues to increase as he is converted.)*

*Conversion is effected by divine forgiveness which remits sins.* The sequence is something like this: An honest seeker hears the message. He asks the Lord in prayer if it is true. The Holy Spirit gives him a witness. This is a testimony. If ones testimony is strong enough, he **repents** and **obeys** the commandments. By such obedience he **receives divine forgiveness which remits sin. Thus, he is converted to a newness of life. His spirit is healed"**…Jesus frequently spoke of his healing the converted. Citing Isaiah, he said, 'This people's heart is waxed gross, and their ears are dull of hearing, and their eyes they have closed; lest at any time they should see with their eyes, and hear with their ears and should understand with their heart, and **should be converted and I should heal them.***(Matt. 13:15)….To the distraught Nephites, he thus spoke out of the awful darkness which attended his crucifixion: 'O all ye that are spared because ye were **more righteous** than they, will ye not now **return unto me, and repent of your sins,** and be **converted, that I may heal you:** *(3 Nephi 9:13)* Somebody recently asked how one could know when by the power of the Holy Spirit his soul is healed. When this occurs, **he will recognize it by the way he feels,** for he will feel as the people of King Benjamin felt when they received remission of sins. The record says, 'The Spirit of the Lord came upon them, and they were **filled with joy, having received a remission of their sins, and having peace of conscience.**' *Mosiah 4:3 "Look to God and Live" pgs. 109-113*

Elder Bruce R. McConkie, in his book "The Millennial Messiah" pp. 98-99 explains, *"True it is that honest truth seekers come to know of the truth and divinity of the Lord's work by the power of the Holy Ghost: they receive a flash of revelation telling them that Jesus is the Lord, that Joseph Smith is his prophet, that the Book of Mormon is the mind and will and voice of the Lord, that the Church of Jesus Christ of Latter-day Saints is the only true and living Church upon the whole earth. They gain a testimony before baptism. But it is* **only after they pledge their all in the cause of Christ that they receive the gift of the Holy Ghost,** *which is the heavenly endowment of which Jesus spoke. Then they receive a fulfillment of the promise:* **"by the power of the Holy**

*Ghost ye may know the truth of all things." (Moroni 10:5) Then they receive the "spirit of revelation," and the Lord tells them in their heart and in their mind whatsoever he will." (D&C 8:1-3)*

In President Ezra Taft Benson's "The Gospel Teacher and His Message" he states, *"Conversion to Jesus Christ and his gospel is more than testimony; it is to be healed spiritually. In Paul's words, It is to partake of the "power of God." A most commendable example of this process is found in the Book of Mormon in the story of Enos. (Enos 8) Enos was spiritually healed. Through His mighty supplications to God, he experienced what the faithful of any dispensation can do, and must experience if they are to see God.*

*First: "They…viewed themselves in their own carnal (worldly) state."*
*Next: "They all cried aloud with one voice saying: O have mercy, and apply the atoning blood of Christ that we may receive forgiveness of sins, and our hearts may be purified… Finally: "After they had spoken these words the Spirit of the Lord came upon them, and they were filled with joy, having received a remission of their sins, and having peace of conscience, because of the exceeding faith which they had in Jesus Christ…(Mosiah 4:2-3)*

*This is the manner by which the saints in all ages have come to be converted, or in the words of the Book of Mormon, changed from their carnal and fallen state, to a state of righteousness, being redeemed of God, becoming his sons and daughters: and thus they became new creatures…" ( Mosiah 27:25,26) This is what is meant by partaking of the Power of God."*

The word convert is defined in Webster's dictionary as, *"to be turned or changed", a converted person; one who has turned from sin to holiness, conversion; a change from one state to another."* The Bible Dictionary is also very insightful in understanding conversion.

As you begin cross-referencing scriptures, it will become self-evident, that the terms "converted", "mighty change" "change of heart", "spiritually reborn" "born again", "born of God", "baptism of fire", "becoming His sons and daughters", "spiritually healed", "made whole", "clean hands and a pure heart", "cleansed from all sin", "saints," "new creatures in Christ", "receiving the Holy Ghost as a constant companion", "being purified" and "sanctified" are all synonyms.

However, being spiritually born of God usually occurs a long time before ones calling and election is made sure. It is important to understand that both of these experiences must be received prior to becoming a translated being. Realizing this will greatly assist your scripture study, and it will help you more clearly understand the words of the prophets and apostles.

In Act 3:19 we are taught to, *"**Repent** ye therefore, and be **converted**, that your **sins may be blotted out**, when the times of refreshing shall come from the presence of the Lord."* and in Psalm 19:7 we read, *"The law of the Lord is perfect, **converting the soul**: the testimony of the Lord is sure, making wise the simple."*

Elder Bruce R. McConkie wrote in "A New Witness for the Articles of Faith" p. 290, *"Question; When do we receive the actual remission of our sins? When are we changed from our carnal and fallen state to a state of righteousness? When do we become clean and pure and spotless so as to be able to dwell with Gods and angels? What is the baptism of fire and of the Holy Ghost?*
Answer: *Sins are remitted **not** in the waters of baptism, as we say in speaking figuratively, but when we receive the Holy Ghost. It is the Holy Spirit of God that erases carnality and **brings us into a state of righteousness**. We become **clean** when we **actually receive the fellowship and companionship of the Holy Ghost**. It is then that sin and dross and **evil are burned out of our souls as though by fire**. The baptism of the Holy Ghost is the baptism of fire. There have been miraculous **occasions** when visible flames enveloped penitent persons, but ordinarily the cleansing power of the Spirit simply dwells, unseen and unheralded, in the hearts of those who have made the Lord their friend. And the Spirit will not dwell in an unclean tabernacle."*

Pres. Joseph Fielding Smith said, *"The Holy Ghost will not dwell in unclean tabernacles or disobedient tabernacles. The Holy Ghost will **not dwell** with that person who is **unwilling to obey** and keep the commandments of God or* *who violates those commandments willingly. In such a soul the spirit of the Holy Ghost cannot enter. That great gift comes to us only through **humility** and **faith** and **obedience**. Therefore, a **great many members** of the Church **do not have that guidance**."* ("Take Heed to Yourselves" p 364, TLDP p. 79)

President Joseph F. Smith proclaimed, *"There is not one that God has not called to repentance, which means the **forsaking of sin**, a departure from evil, to **do righteousness** and walk in the way of life and salvation. I understand that unless we do this we will be **weighed** in the **balance** and **found wanting**."* (CR, Apr. 1880, P.36)

Pres. Joseph F. Smith also wrote, *"Of **what use is it** that we know the truth, **if we lack its spirit? Our knowledge**, in this event, becomes a **condemnation to us, failing to bear fruit**. It is not sufficient that we know the truth, but **we must be humble** and with this knowledge **possess the spirit to actuate us to good deeds**. Baptism, as well as all other outward ordinances, **without the spirit accompanying, is useless. We remain but baptized sinners**. It is the duty of the young men* (and all members) *of Israel to **seek first the Kingdom of God and his righteousness**, and leave other things to follow; to **seek the spirit of truth** so as to possess the knowledge of God, which **giveth them a desire for purity, light, truth**; and a **spirit to despise evil** and to **turn away** from **all** that is **not of God**."* (TLDP 284-285) (parenthesis added)

We are taught by Alma to *"**not procrastinate the day of your repentance**."* (Alma 34:33). **And *"blessed are they who humble themselves without being compelled to be humble;"*** (see Alma 32:16). To those who take the steps, and become spiritually born of God will be spared the anguish, which the Nephites suffered when they cried out, *"**O that we had repented before this great and terrible day…**"* (3 Nephi 8:24.)

In Alma 5:27-31, we hear urgency in Alma's inspired words, *"Have ye walked, **keeping yourselves blameless** before God? Could ye say, if ye were called to die at this time, within yourselves, that ye have been **sufficiently humble**? That your garments have been **cleansed and made white through the blood of Christ**, who will come to redeem his people from their sins? Behold, are ye **stripped of pride**? I say unto you, if ye are not ye are not pre-*

*pared to meet God. Behold ye must prepare quickly; for the kingdom of heaven is soon at hand, and such an one hath not eternal life. Behold, I say, is there one among you who is not **stripped of envy?** I say unto you that such an one is not prepared; and I would that he should **prepare quickly, for the hour is close at hand,** and he knoweth not when the time shall come; for such an one is not found guiltless. And again I say unto you, is there one among you that doth make a **mock of his brother,** or that heapeth upon him persecutions? Wo unto such an one, for he is not prepared, and the **time is at hand that he must repent or he cannot be saved!"***

Remember the Lord can save us from our sins, only if we are truly penitent. He cannot save us **in** our sins, for he is a just God, and mercy cannot rob justice. (See Alma 42:23-26). If we are to stand clean, and spotless before the Lord, we must climb each step required to become worthy, and spiritually ready to be born again. Those who become spiritually born of God, as was Alma, receive a mighty change of heart.

*"And **according to his faith** there was a mighty change wrought in his heart. Behold I say unto you that this is all true. And behold, he preached the word unto your fathers, and a **mighty change was also wrought in their hearts,** and **they humbled themselves and put their trust in the true and living God.** And behold, they were **faithful until the end;** therefore they were saved. And now behold, I ask of you my **brethren (members) of the church, have ye been born of God? Have ye received his image in your countenances?** Have ye **experienced this mighty change** in your hearts? Do ye **exercise faith** in the redemption of him who created you? Do you look forward with an **eye of faith,** and view this mortal body raised in immortality, and this corruption raised in incorruption, to stand before God to be judged according to the deeds which have been done in the mortal body? I say unto you, can you imagine to yourselves that ye hear the voice of the Lord, saying unto you, in that day: Come unto me ye blessed, for behold, your works have been the **works of righteousness** upon the face of the earth? Or **do ye imagine to yourselves that ye can lie unto the Lord** in that day and say-Lord, our works have been righteous works upon the face of the earth-and that he will save you? Or otherwise, can ye imagine yourselves brought before the tribunal of God with your souls filled*

*with guilt and remorse, having a remembrance of all your guilt, yea, **perfect remembrance of all your wickedness**, yea, a remembrance that ye have set at defiance the commandments of God? I say unto you, can ye look up to God at that day with a **pure heart and clean hands**? I say unto you, can you look up, having the **image of God engraven upon your countenances**?…I say unto you, ye will know at that day that ye cannot be saved; for there **can no man be saved except his garments are washed white**; yea, his garments must **be purified until they are cleansed from all stain**, through the blood of him of whom it has been spoken by our fathers, who should come to redeem his people from their sins.*" (Alma 5:12-19, 21)

When Christ appeared to the Nephites, he said, "*O all ye that are spared because ye were more righteous than they, will ye not now return unto me, and **repent** of your sins, and **be converted, that I may heal you**? Yea, verily I say unto you, if ye will come unto me **ye shall have eternal life**. Behold, mine arm of mercy is extended towards you, and whosoever will come, him will I receive; and blessed are those who come unto me.*" (3 Nephi 9:13)

If we are to be spiritually and physically healed, we must receive the mighty change of heart, or the mighty conversion of our hearts. For they "*are sanctified by the Spirit unto the renewing* (and healing) *of their bodies.*" (D&C 84:33) Spiritual healing and physical healing often occur at the same time, as when Jesus told the man with palsy, "*thy sins are forgiven thee.*" and "*…he rose up before them…glorifying God.*" (Luke 5:20-25) The Lord also told Enos, "*thy sins are forgiven thee, and thou shalt be blessed.*" and "*…thy faith hath made thee whole.*" When one is made whole, he is often healed completely, both physically and spiritually.

May the Lord's choice blessing of being converted, and receiving the mighty change of heart, be your greatest desire. That He may heal you, and whisper to your soul "*thy sins are forgiven thee, thy faith hath made thee whole.*"

# CHAPTER 4

# "No More Disposition to Do Evil"

When one has been spiritually born of God, and receives the mighty change of heart, do they lose the disposition, they previously had to sin, or commit transgressions?

In Mosiah 5: 2-5 we read, "*And they all cried with one voice, saying: Yea, we believe all the words which thou hast spoken unto us; and also, we know of their surety and truth, because of the Spirit of the Lord Omnipotent, which has wrought a mighty change in us, or in our hearts, that we have **no more disposition to do evil, but to do good continually.** And we, ourselves, also, through the infinite goodness of God, and the **manifestations of his Spirit**, have great views of that which is to come; and were it expedient, we could prophesy of all things. And it is the faith which we have had on the things which our king has spoken unto us that has brought us to this great knowledge, whereby we do rejoice with such **exceedingly great joy.** And we are willing to enter into a covenant with our God to do his will, and to be obedient to his commandments in all things that he shall command us, all the remainder of our days, that we may not bring upon ourselves a never-ending torment, as has been spoken by the angel, that we may not drink out of the cup of the wrath of God.*"

Elder Bruce R. McConkie wrote in his "Commentary on the Book of Mormon" (Volume 2, p. 78), "*Yes, we believe all the words which thou hast spoken unto us. Great was the joy of King Benjamin when he found that they not only believed his words but also because of the working of the Spirit of the*

Lord in their hearts, they knew of their truth. Still more, the **Holy Spirit had wrought such a change within them** that they had no more disposition to do evil but to **do good continually**. The visions of eternity were **opened to their minds**; their **souls were filled with the spirit** of prophecy, and they longed to **serve the Lord with undivided hearts. Peace, joy, exceeding gladness**, overflowed the confines of their beings. With knowledge and understanding they praised the great name of the Lord. They rehearsed, before Him, His marvelous works, and together they spoke of the glory of His Kingdom, and talked of His might. They exulted in the Lord Omnipotent and rejoiced in the God of their Salvation."

Additional accounts in the Book of Mormon testify of losing any disposition to do evil. In 2 Nephi 9:49, the prophet Nephi tells us, "*Behold, my soul abhorreth sin, and my heart delighteth in righteousness; and I will praise the holy name of my God.*"

The prophet Jacob also testifies of his abhorrence to sin, in Jacob 2:5-7, "*But behold, hearken ye unto me, and know that by the help of the all powerful Creator of heaven and earth I can tell you concerning your thoughts, how that ye are beginning to labor in sin, which **sin appeareth very abominable unto me,** yea, and abominable unto me to shrink with shame before the presence of my Maker, that I must testify unto you concerning the wickedness of your hearts. And also it grieveth me that I must use so much boldness of speech concerning you, before your wives and your children, many of whose feeling are exceedingly tender and chaste and delicate before God, which thing is pleasing unto God;*"

We learn about the people of Anti-Nephi-Lehi, and their abhorrence to sin in Alma 27:27-30, "*And they were among the people of Nephi, and also numbered among the people who were of the church of God. And they were also distinguished for their **zeal towards God**, and also towards men; for they were **perfectly honest** and **upright in all things**; and they were **firm in the faith** of Christ, even unto the end. And they did look upon shedding the blood of their brethren with the **greatest abhorrence;** and they never could be prevailed upon to take up arms against their brethren; and they never did look upon death*"

with any degree of terror, for their hope and views of Christ and the resurrection; therefore, death was swallowed up to them by the victory of Christ over
it. Therefore, they would suffer death in the most aggravating and distressing
manner which could be inflicted by their brethren, before they would take the
sword or cimeter to smite them. And thus they were a **zealous** and **beloved**
people, a highly favored people of the Lord."

Certainly, these people received the mighty change of heart which is given
to all those who have been spiritually born of God. The prophet Joseph
Smith teaches us about losing every desire to sin, when he said, "*We consider that God has created man with a mind capable of instruction, and a fac-
ulty which may be enlarged in proportion to the heed and diligence given to the
light communicated from heaven to the intellect; and that the nearer man
approaches perfection, the* **clearer are his views**, *and the greater his* **enjoy-
ments**, *till he has* **overcome the evils of his life** *and* **lost every desire for sin**;
*and like the ancients, arrives at the point of faith where he is wrapped in the
power and glory of his Maker and is caught up to dwell with Him.*" TPJS:51

President Brigham Young also expands our understanding of being truly
born again, or spiritually born of God; when he said, "*What is it that con-
vinces man? It is the influence of the Almighty,* **enlightening his mind**, *giving
instruction to the understanding. When that inhabits the body, that which
comes from the regions of glory is* **enlightened by the influence, power, and
Spirit of the Father** *of light, it swallows up the organization which pertains to
this world. Those who are governed by this influence* **lose sight** *of all things pertaining to mortality; they are wholly* **influenced by the power of eternity**, *and
lose sight of time. All the honor, wisdom, strength, and whatsoever is* **consid-
ered desirable among men**, *yea, all that pertains to this organization, which is
in any way independent of that which came from the Father of our spirits, is*
**obliterated to them** *and they hear and* **understand** *by the same power and
spirit that clothe the Deity, and the holy beings in His presence…*" (JD1:90.)

In the Book of Mormon, we learn of an entire nation of people, who
received the mighty change of heart. For approximately 166 years they
turned away from all that was not of God. The marvelous account of the

great blessings they received, are summarized in 4 Nephi 1:15-16, "*And it came to pass that there was no contention in the land, because of the **love of God** which did dwell in the hearts of the people. And there were no envyings, nor strifes, nor tumults, nor whoredoms, nor lyings, nor murders, nor any manner of lasciviousness; and surely there could not be a **happier** people among all the people who had been created by the hand of God.*" (Certainly, these righteous Nephites were blessed with the constant companionship of the Holy Spirit) "*which giveth them a desire for purity, light, truth; and a spirit to despise evil and to turn away from all that is not of God.*" (quoted earlier in text by Joseph F. Smith)

So one might ask, does this mean that one who has been spiritually born of God, will never make mistakes, commit transgressions, or sins? In the Doctrine and Covenants 20:33-34 we read, "*Therefore let the church take heed and pray always, lest they fall into temptation; Yea, and even **let those who are sanctified take head also**.*" These verses clearly explain that there are **some** members of the church who have received the marvelous blessing of becoming sanctified. They need to take heed also and prayer always, so that they will not fall into temptation.

The prophet Joseph Smith and Oliver Cowdery experienced this marvelous event, of being spiritually born of God, at the same time. Joseph Smith-History verse 73, it reads, "*Immediately on our coming up out of the water after we had been baptized, we experienced great and glorious blessings from our Heavenly Father. No sooner had I baptized Oliver Cowdery, than the **Holy Ghost fell upon him**, and he stood up and **prophesied** many things which should shortly come to pass. And again, so soon as I had been baptized by him, I also had **the spirit** of prophecy, when, standing up, I prophesied concerning the rise of this Church, and many other things connected with the Church, and this generation of the children of men. We were **filled with the Holy Ghost**, and rejoiced in the God of our salvation.*"

After having been baptized with fire and the Holy Ghost, Joseph was made spotless before the Lord, and he had undoubtedly lost all disposition to do evil. However, he was still a mortal man and he occasionally transgressed, such as when he gave the 116 pages of manuscript to Martin Harris.

Nephi is another example of a great prophet, who in the depths of humility, confessed his sin of being angry with his brethren. Was Nephi just depressed and had turned his anger inward, against himself? Or was it because of Nephi's vivid awareness of the Lord's standard of righteousness, that he repents with all the sincerity of his heart when he said, "*Nevertheless, notwithstanding the great goodness of the Lord, in showing me his great and marvelous works, my heart exclaimeth: O wretched man that I am! Yea, my heart sorroweth because of my flesh; my soul grieveth because of mine iniquities. I am encompassed about, because of the temptations and the sins which do so easily beset me. And when I desire to rejoice, my heart groaneth because of my sins; nevertheless, I know in whom I have trusted. My God hath led me through mine afflictions in the wilderness; and he hath preserved me upon the waters of the great deep. **He hath filled me with his love,** even unto the consuming of my flesh.*" (2 Nephi 4:17-21)

Isn't it possible that two of Nephi's reasons for including these verses, were first, to show us how to come to the Lord with a broken, penitent heart; and second, to remind us that even the sanctified, make mistakes and need repentance. Even those who have lost all disposition to do evil, will at times transgress Gods laws, and because they also have a great desire to do good continually, they will speedily repent, if they are wise.

Each of the scriptural accounts quoted, clearly show us that when one has been spiritually born of God, he loses all disposition to do evil, to transgress, or to commit even minor sins. In fact, even the appearance of sin becomes an abhorrence to one who has received the mighty change of heart. Certainly, there is a marvelous change which occurs in the hearts of those who have been born again. A change which will be perceived, felt and eventually understood by one who has received it. A change which is like the wind, as Jesus said to Nicodemus, "*The wind bloweth where it listeth, and thou hearest the sound thereof, but canst not tell whence it cometh, and whither it goeth: so is ever one that is born of the Spirit.*" (John 3:8)

# CHAPTER 5

# "By the Blood Ye are Sanctified"

President Brigham Young gave us a powerful statement on sanctification when he said, *"I will put my own definition to the term sanctification, and say it consists in overcoming every sin and bringing all into subjection to the law of Christ. God has placed in us a pure spirit; when this reigns predominant, without let or hindrance, and* **triumphs over the flesh** *and rules and governs and controls as the Lord controls the heavens and the earth, this I call the blessing of sanctification. Will sin be perfectly destroyed? No it will not, for it is not so designed in the economy of Heaven…"* (TLDP:604)

President Young also said, *"When the will, passions and feelings of a person are perfectly submissive to God and His requirements, that person is* **sanctified***. It is for* **my will** *to be* **swallowed up** *in the* **will of God,** *that will lead me into all good, and crown me ultimately with immortality and eternal lives."* (JD2:123)

Also in the Journal of Discourses 9:288, President Brigham Young stated, *"When through the Gospel the Spirit in man has so* **subdued the flesh** *that he* **can live without willful transgression, the Spirit of God unites with his spirit, they become congenial companions,** *and the* **mind** *and* **will of the creator is thus transmitted** *to the* **creature.***"*

In Alma 13:10-13 we read, *"Now, as I said concerning the holy order, or this high priesthood, there were* **many** *who were ordained and became high priests* *of God; and it was on account of their **exceeding faith and repentance**, and their **righteousness** before God, they choosing to **repent** and **work righteousness** rather than to perish; Therefore they were called after this holy order, and were **sanctified**, and their **garments** were washed **white** through the **blood of the Lamb**. Now they, after being sanctified by the Holy Ghost, having their garments made white, being pure and spotless before God, could not look upon **sin** save it were with **abhorrence**; and there were many, **exceedingly great many**, who were made pure and entered into the rest of the Lord their God. And now, my brethren, I would that ye should humble yourselves before God, and bring forth fruit meet for repentance, that ye may also enter into that rest."*

These verses clearly teach us that there can be **many people, made spotless** before the Lord, while they are still in this life. Jesus teaches us of the absolute necessity of becoming sanctified when he said, *"And no unclean thing can enter into his kingdom; therefore nothing entereth into his rest save it be those who have washed their garments in my blood, because of their faith, and the repentance of **all** their sins, and their faithfulness unto the end. Now this is the commandment: Repent, all ye ends of the earth, and come unto me and be baptized in my name, that ye **may be sanctified by the reception of the Holy Ghost**, that ye **may** stand spotless before me at the last day. Verily, verily, I say unto you **this is my gospel;**"* (3 Nephi 27:19-21)

In D&C 76:40-41, *"And **this is the gospel**, the glad tidings, which the voice out of the heavens bore record unto us-That he came unto the world, even Jesus, to be crucified for the world, and to bear the sins of the world, and to **sanctify** the world, and to cleanse it from all unrighteousness;"*

The Lord tells us that **this** is His gospel. **This** is what everything in the gospel points us towards, becoming sanctified and able to stand spotless before him. *"For behold **this** is my work and my glory to bring to pass the immortality and eternal life of man."* (Moses 1:39)

In the D&C 39:6, *"**And this is my gospel**-repentance and baptism by water, and then cometh the **baptism of fire** and the Holy Ghost, even the Comforter, which **showeth all things**, and **teacheth** the peaceable things of the kingdom."*

In Moses 6:59-60 we read, *"That by reason of transgression cometh the fall, which fall bringeth death, and inasmuch as ye were born into the world by the water, and blood, and the spirit, which I have made, and so became of dust a living soul, even so ye* **must be born again into the kingdom of heaven,** *of* **water,** *and of the* **Spirit,** *and* **be cleansed by blood,** *even the blood of mine Only Begotten; that ye* **might be sanctified from all sin,** *and enjoy the words of eternal life in this world, and eternal life in the world to come, even immortal glory; For by the water ye keep the commandment; by the* **Spirit ye are justified,** *and by the* **blood are sanctified;"**

In both the physical and the spiritual birth there is a process, and eventually an event. In the physical, the mother experiences many discomforts, and it is usually the longest nine months of her life. For the unborn infant it is a time of rapid growth. So it is with the spiritual rebirth, there must be time for us to grow in our righteousness. The difficult and uncomfortable times of life, are when we typically experience the most rapid spiritual growth. And just as the unborn baby needs time to grow, we each need time to grow spiritually.

Finally, when we become spiritually ready (as an unborn baby needs to be physically ready), we turn to the Lord, and truly come unto Him. Praying with all the sincerity of our hearts, and fasting often, with real intent, confessing all of our sins to God, with a broken heart and a contrite spirit in godly sorrow, for having caused such terrible pain to come upon our beloved Savior. If we then totally submit our lives to the Lord, and say "not my will, but thy will be done." Then in the Lord's own due time, and usually when our souls are in the mist of travail, our Savior delivers us from evil. He delivers us from our sins, and completely forgives us, then we are cleansed by his precious, atoning blood. We are made pure and spotless, clean every wit. The event of spiritual birth happens! We become sons and daughters of Christ! (Mosiah 5:7) He has spiritually begotten us! We are born again, and we experience a newness of life. We become new creatures in Christ, because the old man of sin dies, we have put off the natural man and have become true saints, (See 1 Corinthians 1:2) with no more deposition to do evil, but to do good continually. We are filled with exceeding great joy!

Because we are filled with the Holy Ghost! For we have been baptized by fire and by the Holy Ghost!

The same three elements of the water, the spirit and the blood are present at both the physical and the spiritual birth. The water—is of course the waters of baptism. The Spirit—is the Holy Spirit which justifies, or witnesses that this person is defensible, that his repentance is complete, and he becomes justifiable before God.(see Moses 6:60) The blood, is the atoning blood of Jesus Christ, which when applied by the Lord, cleanses one from all sin and sanctifies him..

In Mosiah 5:7 we read, *"And now, because of the covenant which ye have made ye shall be called the **children of Christ**, his sons, and his daughters; for behold, this day he hath **spiritually begotten you;** for ye say that your hearts are **changed through faith** on his name; therefore, ye are born of him and have become **his sons and his daughters."***

There are several places in the scriptures where the steps to sanctification are identified. At the very end of the Book of Mormon we are given a marvelous summary in Moroni 10:32-33, *"Yea, **come unto Christ,** and be perfected in him, and **deny yourselves of all ungodliness;** and if ye shall deny yourselves of all ungodliness, and **love God with all your might, mind** and **strength, then is his grace sufficient for you,** that by his grace ye may be perfect in Christ; and if by the grace of God ye are perfect in Christ, ye can in nowise deny the power of God. And again, if ye by the **grace of God are perfect in Christ,** and deny not his power, then are ye **sanctified in Christ** by the grace of God, through the shedding of the **blood of Christ,** which is in the covenant of the Father unto the **remission of your sins, that ye become holy, without spot."***

Helaman 3:35 states, *"Nevertheless they did **fast and pray oft,** and did wax stronger and stronger in their **humility** and firmer and firmer in the **faith** of Christ, unto the **filling their souls with joy** and consolation, yea, even to the **purifying** and the **sanctification** of their hearts, which sanctification cometh because of their **yielding their hearts unto God."***

D&C 93:1 reads, *"Verily, thus saith the Lord: It shall come to pass that every soul who (1) forsaketh his sins and (2) cometh unto me, and (3)calleth on my name, (4) and obeyeth my voice, and (5) keepeth my commandments, shall see my face and know that I am;"* (Numbers 1-5 added)

In each of these principles, total commitment is required, if we are to receive these marvelous blessings. (1) Totally forsaking and confessing all of our sins to God, with a broken heart, grieving over the suffering we have caused our beloved Savior. (2) Truly coming to Christ, in mighty prayer, by opening the door to our hearts and letting Him in. Learning to love the Lord with all of our hearts, minds and strength, and loving our neighbor as ourselves. For as we have done it unto the least of these…we have done it unto Him. (3) Praying with all the energy of our hearts, "with real intent, having faith in Jesus Christ." (Moroni 9:4) Praying continually, without ceasing and striving to direct our thoughts to the Lord unceasingly. (4) Striving to live "by every word the proceedeth from the mouth of God." Matt 4:4 And (5) Keeping all of the commandments, because we love Him.

The commandments are truths, and "the truth shall make us free." John 8:32 So when we keep the commandments, we are keeping the truths that shall free us from the consequences of sin.  Each time we choose to obey a commandment, we choose to love and serve the Lord, instead of the world, if we obey with a willing heart.

In 1 Thessalonians 5:15-23, we are given more instructions, in the principles of the gospel which if obeyed, will lead us towards sanctification." *See that none render evil for evil unto any man; but ever (1) **follow that which is good**, both among yourselves, and to all men. (2) **Rejoice evermore.** (3) **Pray without ceasing.** (4) **In every thing give thanks:** for this is the will of God in Christ Jesus concerning you. (5) **Quench not the Spirit. Despise not prophesyings. (6) Prove all things; hold fast that which is good. (7) Abstain from all appearance of evil.** And the very God of peace **sanctify you wholly;** and I pray God your whole spirit and soul and body be preserved **blameless** unto the coming of our Lord Jesus Christ.* (numbers 1-7 added)

In Hebrew 10:14 it reads, *"For by one offering he (Christ) hath **perfected** for ever them that are **sanctified.**"* (parenthesis added)

2 Timothy 2:21, *"If a man therefore purge himself from these, (ungodliness) he shall be a vessel unto honor, **sanctified**, and meet for the master's use, and prepared unto every good work."* (parenthesis added)

Elder Mark E. Peterson wrote, *"Through righteous living we invite the Holy Spirit in, **when it enters our bodies it sanctifies them with a holy influence** and prepares us for the **spiritual blessings which may be enjoyed by the faithful.** The principle of **sanctification** is one with which many Latter-day Saints are unfamiliar, yet one which **everyone should study**, for the Lord commands us to **sanctify ourselves "that your minds become single to God**, and the days will come that you shall see him, for he will unveil his face unto you, and it shall be in his own time and according to his own will."* (D&C 88:68) *On the day the Church was organized the Lord told the Prophet Joseph Smith that "**sanctification** through the **grace** of our Lord and **Savior Jesus Christ** is just and true, to all those who **love** and **serve God** with **all** their might, minds and strength."* D&C 20:31 *But unless our bodies are clean and ready for the **Holy Spirit** to enter, **it cannot sanctify them,** and **without sanctification, can we be admitted to His presence?**"* (Why the Religious Life? pp 252-53)

Elder Bruce R. McConkie said, *"To be **sanctified is to be cleansed** from all sin; it is to stand **pure and spotless** before the Lord; it is to overcome the world and be a fit candidate for a celestial inheritance. The **"sanctified" are "them of the celestial world.**"* (D&C 88:2) *The Holy Ghost is a sanctifier. His baptism of fire burns dross and evil out of repentant souls as though by fire. Sanctification **comes only** to the **obedient**; it is the truth of heaven-the very word of God, his everlasting gospel-which sanctifies the souls of men."* (The Mortal Messiah, 4:114)

Elder Delbert L. Stapley, in Oct. conference 1966 stated that, *"Man can only become **spotless** and **sanctified** by the reception of the Holy Ghost in his personal life. The Holy Ghost is a cleansing and purifying agent to all who receive it and are righteous. This means that **sin** and **iniquity** are **spiritually burned out** of the **repentant person**. He then **receives a remission of sins,** and his **soul*** *is sanctified and made **clean** for the **Holy Ghost to abide in him. The cleansed person enjoys a newness of life** and **becomes a new creature in the spirit.**"*

Elder Joseph Fielding Smith (later became President of the Church) said, *"Sanctification is also true. Through the praise of the Father, we may be **sanctified from all sin** through acceptance of the Gospel and compliance with all the ordinances. We are told that those "who overcome by faith, and are sealed by the Holy Spirit of promise, which the father sheds forth upon all those who are **just and true" will be entitled to become sons of God.**"* (See D&C 76:53-54) CHMR 1:94

Elder Orson Pratt said, *"We believe in the sanctification that comes by continued obedience to the law of heaven. I do not know of any other sanctification that the Scriptures tell about, of any other sanctification that is worth the consideration of rational beings. If we would be sanctified then, we must begin today, or whenever the Lord points out, to **obey his laws just as far as we possible can;** and by obedience to these laws we continually gain more and more favor from heaven, more and **more of the Spirit of God,** and thus will be fulfilled a revelation given in 1834, which says that before Zion is redeemed, let the armies of Israel become very great, let them become **sanctified** before me; that they may be as fair as the sun, clear as the moon, and that their banners may be terrible unto all the nations of the earth-not terrible by reason of numbers, but **terrible** because of the **sanctification** they will receive through obedience to the law of God. Why was Enoch, and why were the inhabitants of Zion built up before the terrible flood to all the nations around about? It was because, through a long number of years, they observed the law of God, and when their enemies came up to fight against them, Enoch, being **filled** with the power of the Holy Ghost, and speaking the **word of God in power and in faith,** the very heavens trembled and shook, and the earth quaked, and mountains were thrown down, rivers of water were turned out of their course, and all nations feared greatly because of the power of God, and the **terror of his might** that were upon his people.* (Moses 7: 12-17). *We have this account of ancient Zion in one of the revelations that God has given. What was it that made their banners terrible to the nations? It was not their numbers. If, then **Zion must become great it will be because of her sanctification.**"* (JD, 17:112, LDPDC: 456-57)

Isaiah 13:2-3, *"Lift ye up a banner upon the high mountain, exalt the voice unto them, shake the hand, that they may go into the gates of the nobles. I have commanded my **sanctified ones,** I have also called my mighty ones for mine anger, even them that rejoice in my highness."*

Ezekiel 38:16, *"And thou shalt come up against my people of Israel, as a cloud to cover the land; it shall be in the **latter days,** and I will bring thee against my land, that the heathen may know me, when I shall be **sanctified in thee,** O Gog, before their eyes."*

I would like to invite you to reread all of D&C 45. May I quote just a few verse here, D&C 45:57, 70-71, *"For they that are wise and have received the truth, and have **taken the Holy Spirit for their guide,** and have not been deceived-verily I say unto you, they **shall not be hewn down** and cast into the fire, but shall abide the day...And it shall be said among the wicked: Let us not go up to battle against Zion, for the inhabitants of Zion are **terrible;** wherefore we cannot stand. And it shall come to pass that the righteous shall be gathered out from among all nations, and shall come to **Zion, singing with songs of everlasting joy."***

The sanctified will seem terrible to the wicked, because of the power of God which will be in them. However, the righteous need not fear, because the pure in heart, the sanctified, will be protected and will sing with exceeding great joy! Some additional scriptures, which teach us concerning those who will abide the great day of the Lord, are: D&C 45:37-40, 57,61-63 J.S. Matt. 1:14-17, 20, 23, 29, 34, 38-43, 47-55; 1 Thess. 5: 2-10; D&C 38:29-31; D&C 29:6-10; D&C 63:34; D&C 38:42; D&C 76:9-10; Hebrews 11:17; 2 Nephi 32:3.

The Lord will bless and protect his saints, no matter what trials will be placed before them. The word "saint" and the word "sanctified" both come from the Latin word "sanctus" meaning **holy,** and **consecrated.** Therefore, a true saint is one who has become sanctified. You may want to look up "saint" in the Bible Dictionary. It tells us that a saint must be without blemish. May we always strive to live free from all blemishes, sins and transgressions, by humbly repenting each day and confessing all of our sins to the Lord, with a broken heart and contrite spirit, and by consecrating our lives to the Lord. So that by the Holy Spirit, we may be justified, then by our beloved Savior's atoning blood we may be sanctified. (Moses 6:60) and become true saints, holy, sanctified and washed clean in the blood of the Lamb of God.

CHAPTER 6

# "Gifts of the Spirit"

When you have been spiritually born of God, will you recognize that you have received additional spiritual gifts? The Prophet Joseph Smith gave this instruction on June 27, 1839. *"There are two Comforters spoken of. One is the Holy Ghost, the same as given on the day of Pentecost, and that all Saints receive after faith, repentance, and baptism. This **first Comforter or Holy Ghost** has no other effect than **pure intelligence.** It is more powerful in **expanding the mind, enlightening the understanding,** and storing the intellect with present knowledge, of a man who is of the literal seed of Abraham, than one that is a Gentile, though it may not have half as much visible effect upon the body; for as the Holy Ghost falls upon one of the literal seed of Abraham, it is **calm and serene; and his whole soul and body are only exercised by the pure spirit of intelligence;** while the effect of the Holy Ghost upon a Gentile, is to purge out the old blood, and make him actually of the seed of Abraham. The man that has none of the blood of Abraham naturally must have a new creation by the Holy Ghost. In such a case there may be more of a powerful effect upon the body, and visible to the eye, than upon an Israelite, while the Israelite at first might be far before the Gentile in pure intelligence."* (TPJS: 140-50)

In the "Key to Science of Theology" p.16 Elder Parley P. Pratt wrote, *"The gift of the Holy Ghost...quickens all the intellectual faculties, increases, enlarges, expands, and purifies all the natural passions and affections, and adapts them, by the gift of wisdom, to their lawful use. It inspires, develops, cultivates, and matures all the fine-tones sympathies, joys, tastes, kindred feelings, and affections of our nature. It inspires virtue, kindness, goodness, tenderness, gentleness, and charity. It develops beauty of person, form, and features. It tends to health, vigor, animation, and social feeling. It invigorates all the faculties of the physical and intellectual man. It strengthens and gives tone to the nerves. In short, it is, as it were, marrow to the bone, joy to the heart, light to the eyes, music to the ears, and life to the whole being."* (DGSM p. 45)

President John Taylor said, *"When you get the Spirit of God, you feel full of kindness, charity, long-suffering, and you are willing all the day long to accord to every man that which you want yourself. You feel disposed all the day long to do unto all men as you would wish them to do unto you."* (JD, May 18, 1862, 10:57)

Pres. Taylor also said, *"Now, what did Jesus tell His disciples the Holy Ghost should do when it came? He promised-"It shall lead you into all truth" What shall it do?*

*Lead you into all truth-not into a diversity of sentiments, not into differences of doctrine, not into a variety of ordinances, but you shall see alike, comprehend alike and understand alike. "It shall lead you unto all truth."* (JD 23:374) In Moroni 10:5 we read: *"And by the power of the Holy Ghost ye may know the truth of all things."*

President Brigham Young taught us that, *"The Holy Ghost reveals unto you things past, present, and to come; it makes your minds quick and vivid to understand the handiwork of the Lord. Your joy is made full in beholding the footsteps of our Father going forth among the inhabitants of the earth; this is not visible to the world, but it is made visible to the Saints, and they behold the Lord in his providences, bringing forth the work of the last days."* (JD 4:22)

President Young also said, *"Our faith is concentrated in the Son of God, and through him in the Father; and the Holy Ghost is their minister to bring truths to our remembrance, to reveal new truths to us, and teach, guide, and direct the course of every mind, until we become perfected and prepared to go home, where we can see and converse with our Father in Heaven."* (JD 6:98)

The Lord, himself tells us in John 14:26-27, *"But the Comforter, which is the Holy Ghost, whom the Father will send in my name, he shall **teach you all things,** and bring all **things to your remembrance,** whatsoever I have said unto you. Peace I leave with you, my peace I give unto you; not as the world giveth, give I unto you. Let not your heart be troubled, neither let it be afraid."*

Elder George Q. Cannon gives us additional insights to the wonderful spiritual gifts that may be enjoyed by those who have been spiritually born of God. *"The only way to maintain our position in the Kingdom of God is to so conduct ourselves that we may have a living testimony of the truth continually dwelling in our bosoms, to live so that the **Spirit of the Lord may be a constant and abiding** quest with us, whether in the privacy of our chamber, in the domestic circle or in the midst of the crowded thoroughfares, the busy scenes and anxious cares of life. He who will pursue this course will **never lack for knowledge;** he will never be in **doubt or in darkness, nor will his mind ever be clouded by the gloomy pall of unbelief;** on the contrary **his hopes will be bright; his faith will be strong; his joy will be full;** he will be able each succeeding day to **comprehend the unfolding purposes of Jehovah** and to **rejoice in the glorious liberty and happiness** which all the faithful children of God enjoy…We can only retain the testimony of the truth in our heart by **living near unto God.** If we call upon Him in faith to bless us and **seek to enjoy the companionship of the Holy Spirit,** so ordering our lives that God can, consistently, bless us and the **Spirit of the Lord can abide with us,** we receive **strength to over come every evil and our minds instinctively recoil from the commission of any act which might grieve that Spirit or bring a stain** upon our own character or upon the divine cause in which we are engaged."* (Gospel Truth 1:343-344)

Elder John A Widtsoe wrote, *"…When the servants of the Lord display a **spiritual power** beyond the command of man; when the grief laden heart beats with **joy;** when failure is converted into **victory, it is by the visitation of the Holy Ghost.** It is the Spirit of God under the direction of the Holy Ghost that quickeneth all things. The **gift of the Holy Ghost remains inoperative unless a person leads a blameless life."* (TLDP: 276-277)

Elder Bruce R. McConkie, in his book "The Millennial Messiah" p. 98-99 reaffirms the difference between being "confirmed" or invited to receive the Holy Ghost, and actually receiving the Holy Ghost as a constant companion. *"True it is that honest truth seekers come to know of the truth and divinity of the Lord's work by the power of the Holy Ghost; they receive a flash of revelation telling them that Jesus is the Lord, that Joseph Smith is his prophet,... They gain a testimony before baptism. But it is **only after they pledge their all in the cause of Christ that they receive the gift of the Holy Ghost**, which is the heavenly endowment of which Jesus spoke. **Then** they receive a fulfillment of the promise: "by the power of the Holy Ghost ye may know the truth of all things"* Moroni 10:5. ***Then** they receive the **"spirit of revelation"** and the Lord tells them in their heart and in their mind whatsoever he will."*

Elder Joseph Fielding Smith in Doctrines of Salvation 1:39 he wrote, *"We know what has been revealed and that the Holy Ghost, sometimes spoken of as the Holy Spirit, and Comforter, is the third member of the Godhead, and that he, being in perfect harmony with the Father and the Son, reveals to man by the spirit of revelation and prophecy the truths of the gospel of Jesus Christ. Our great duty is so **to live that we may be led constantly in light and truth by this Comforter** so that we may not be deceived by the many false spirits that are in the world."*

Elder Orson F. Whitney told about his spiritual rebirth, and the gifts that came to him, in April Conference 1930 p.134-135, when he said, *"Anything that furnishes evidence that this is God's work, is a testimony concerning it. But healings are not the greatest evidence-they are but parts of a supreme testimony, greater than dreams, visions, prophecies, healings, tongues, and all other manifestations combined. The **greatest of all testimonies is the illumination of the soul by the gift and power of the Holy Ghost**. How well I remember **when it came to me**. It showed me my place in the divine scheme of things; it showed me where I came from, why I am here, what is expected of me while I am here, and what awaits me in the Great Hereafter. **This is the greatest thing that God ever did for me**."* (LDPDC 3:92)

Elder James E. Talmage in "The Articles of Faith" p. 147 wrote, *"The office of* the Holy Ghost in His ministrations among those **who are entitled** to His tuition He will **reveal all thing necessary** for the soul's advancement. Through the influences of the Holy Spirit the powers of the human **mind** may be **quickened** and increased, so that things past may be brought to remembrance. He will serve as a **guide** in things divine unto all who **will obey Him,** enlightening every man, in the measure of his **humility and obedience; unfolding the mysteries of God,** as the knowledge thus revealed may effect **greater spiritual growth; conveying knowledge from God** to man; **sanctifying those who have been cleansed through obedience** to the requirements of the Gospel, **manifesting** all things; and **bearing witness** unto men concerning the existence and infallibility of the Father and the Son. Not alone does the **Holy Ghost bring to mind the past** and explain the things of the **present,** but His power is manifested in **prophecy concerning the future.** "He will shew you things to come," declared the Savior to the apostles in promising the advent of the Comforter. Adam, the first prophet of earth, under the influence of the Holy Ghost "predicted whatsoever should befall his posterity unto the latest generation." The power of the Holy Ghost then, is the **spirit of prophecy** and **revelation;** His office is that of **enlightenment of the mind, quickening** of the **intellect, and sanctification of the soul."**

In Moroni 8:25-26 we read, "And the first fruits of repentance is baptism; and baptism cometh by faith unto the fulfilling the commandments and the **fulfilling the commandments bringeth remission of sins;** And the remission of sins bringeth meekness, and lowliness of heart; and **because of meekness and lowliness of heart** cometh the **visitation of the Holy Ghost,** which Comforter filleth with **hope** and **perfect love,** which love endureth by **diligence unto prayer,** until the end shall come, when all the **saints** shall dwell with God."

The Prophet Moroni gave us these inspired words, "And again, behold I say unto you that he cannot have faith and hope, save he shall be meek, and lowly of heart. If so, his faith and hope is vain, for **none is acceptable before God, save the meek** and **lowly in heart;** and if a man be meek and lowly in heart, and confesses by the power of the Holy Ghost that Jesus is the Christ, he must needs have charity; for if he have not charity he is nothing; wherefore he must needs have charity. And charity suffereth long, and is kind, and envieth not, *and is not puffed up, seeketh not her own, is not easily provoked, thinketh no evil, and rejoiceth not in iniquity but rejoiceth in the truth, beareth all things, believeth all things, hopeth all things, endureth all things. Wherefore, my beloved brethren, **if ye have not charity, ye are nothing**, for charity never faileth. Wherefore, cleave unto charity, which is the greatest of all, for all things must fail-But charity is the pure love of Christ, and it endureth forever; and whoso is found possessed of it at the last day, it shall be well with him. Wherefore, my beloved brethren, **pray unto the Father with all the energy of heart,** that ye may be **filled with this love,** which he hath **bestowed** upon all who are **true followers** of his Son, Jesus Christ; that ye **may become the sons of God;** that when he shall appear we shall be like him, for we shall see him as he is; that we may have this hope; that we **may be purified even as he is pure.** Amen.* (Moroni 7:43-48)

President Brigham Young taught, "*...the Spirit that shall come unto you through obedience, which will make you feel like little children, and cause you to **delight in doing good,** to **love your Father in Heaven** and the society of the **righteous...**you will feel a **glow, as of fire, burning within you**; and if you open your mouths to talk you will declare ideas which you did not formerly think of; they will **flow into your mind,** even such as you have not thought of for years.*" (JD 3:211)

In 1 John 4:12-19, we learn more about the perfect love which is given to those who have been born again or have spiritually been born of God. "*...If we love one another, God dwelleth in us, and **his love is perfected** in us. Hereby know we that we dwell in him, and he in us, because he hath **given us of his Spirit.** And we have seen and do testify that the Father sent the Son to be the Savior of the world. Whosoever shall **confess** that Jesus is the Son of God, God dwelleth in him, and he in God. And we have known and believed the **love that God hath to us.** God is love; and **he that dwelleth in love dwelleth in God, and God in him. Herein is our love made perfect, that we may have boldness in the day of judgment: because as he is so are we in this world.** There is no fear in love; but **perfect love casteth out fear:** because fear hath tor-ment. **He that feareth is not made perfect in love. We love him, because he first loved us. If a man say, I love God,** and hateth his brother, he is a liar: for* *he that loveth not his brother whom he hath seen, how can he love God whom he hath not seen? And this commandment have we from him, that **he who loveth God love his brother also.**"*

As you read the epistle of 1&2 John, remember that the Apostle John was speaking mainly to the true saints, the sanctified. When we understand to whom he was teaching, and we study by the faith of the Spirit, then his words can come alive to us. The several gifts of the Spirit are beautiful listed in Galatians 5: 22-25, *"But the fruit of the Spirit is **love, joy, peace, long-suffering, gentleness, goodness, faith, meekness, temperance:** against such there is no law. And they that are Christ's have crucified the flesh with affections and lust. **If we live in the Spirit, let us also walk in the Spirit.**"*

When we have been born of the Spirit, we have "entered in at the gate" (Matt 7:13-14). To press forward along the straight and narrow path, we must pray continually and keep all of the commandments, so the Holy Spirit may be our constant companion. If we do these things, we will continue to grow spiritually and be blessed with additional spiritual gifts. Then we will not only "live in the Spirit," but we will "also walk in the Spirit".

In the Doctrine and Covenants 46:17-26, additional gifts of the spirit are recorded. *"And again, verily I say unto you, to some is given, by the Spirit of God, the **word of wisdom.** To another is given the **word of knowledge,** that all may be taught to be wise and to have knowledge. And again, to some it is given to have **faith to be healed;** And to others it is given to have **faith to heal.** And again, to some is given the **working of miracles;** And to others it is given to **prophesy;** And to others the **discerning of spirits.** And again, it is given to some to speak with **tongues;** And to another is given the **interpretation of tongues.** And all these gifts come from God, for the benefit of the children of God"*

We hear the prophet Moroni's warning to us, if spiritual gifts cease, *"Behold I say unto you, Nay; for it is by faith that miracles are wrought; and it is by faith that angels appear and minister unto men; wherefore, if **these things have ceased wo be unto the children of men,** for it is because of **unbelief,** and* *all is vain. For no man can be saved, according to the words of Christ, save they shall have faith in his name; wherefore, if these things have ceased,* **then has faith ceased also***; and awful is the state of man, for they are as though there had been* **no redemption made.** *But behold, my beloved brethren, I judge better things of you, for I judge that ye have faith in Christ because of your meekness; for if ye have not faith in him then ye are not fit to be numbered among the people of his church."* Moroni 7:37-39.

Elder James E. Talmage summarizes the gifts of the Spirit, when he said, *"As already pointed out, the special office of the Holy Ghost is to* **enlighten** *and* **ennoble** *the mind, to* **purify** *and* **sanctify** *the soul, to* **incite to do good works,** *and to* **reveal the things of God.** *But, beside these general blessings, there are certain* **specific endowments promised in connection with the gifts of the Holy Ghost.** *The Savior said: 'These signs shall follow them that believe; In my name shall they cast out devils; they shall speak with new tongues; They shall take up serpents; and if they drink any deadly thing, it shall not hurt them; they shall lay hands on the sick, and they shall recover.' These* **gifts** *of the Spirit are* **distributed** *in the wisdom of God for the* **salvation** *of His children..."* (AF 151-152

# CHAPTER 7

# *"My Guilt was Swept Away"*

Is it important to have the Spirit witness to us that all of our guilt is swept away, while we are still in this life? In Alma 11:43 we read, "…and *we shall be brought to stand before God knowing even as we know now, and have a bright **recollection of all our guilt**." and in Alma 5:18, "…can ye imagine yourselves brought before the tribunal of God with your souls filled with guilt and remorse, having a remembrance of **all your guilt,** yea, a perfect remembrance of all your wickedness, yea, a remembrance that ye have set at defiance the commandments of God?*

Remember that the Lord's definition of wickedness is not the same as our typical use of the word wicked. *"For I the Lord cannot look upon sin with the least degree of allowance;"* (see D&C 1:31 and Alma 45:16.) We also learn in 2 Nephi 9:14, "*Wherefore, we shall have a **perfect knowledge of all our guilt**, and our uncleanness, and our nakedness; and the **righteous** shall have a **perfect knowledge** of their **enjoyment**, and their **righteousness**, being clothed with **purity**, yea, even with the robe of righteousness."*

Moroni teaches us these same truths in Mormon 9: 3-6, "*…Do ye suppose that ye shall dwell with him under a consciousness of your guilt? Do ye suppose that ye could be happy to dwell with that holy Being, when your souls are racked with a consciousness of guilt that ye have ever abused his laws? Behold, I say unto you that ye would be more miserable to dwell with a holy and just God, under a **consciousness of your filthiness** before him, than ye would to dwell with the damned souls in hell. For behold, when he shall be brought to see your nakedness before God, and also the glory of God, and the holiness of*

*Jesus Christ, it will kindle a flame of unquenchable fire upon you. O then ye unbelieving, turn ye unto the Lord;* **cry mightily** *unto the Father in the name of Jesus, that perhaps ye may be found* **spotless, pure, fair, and white, having been cleansed by the blood of the Lamb,** *at that great and last day."*

Since we have all sinned, we will have a perfect remembrance of all our guilt, unless, we have come to the Lord with a broken heart, and a contrite spirit, and have confessed all of our sins to God, asking Him, in total humility to forgive us. Fasting often and praying continually, with all the energy of our hearts that our faith, hope and love my increase. Striving to *"live by every word that proceedeth from the mouth of God."* (D&C 84:44) Only then can the Spirit justify us, and our Savior's precious atoning blood sanctify us, and make us spotless, and clean every whit. (Moses 6:60)

The wonderful testimony of Enos, assists in our understanding of full repentance, and the marvelous blessing of having one's guilt totally swept away. *"And my soul* **hungered;** *and I kneeled down before my maker, and I* **cried** *unto him in* **mighty prayer** *and supplication for mine* **own soul;** *and all the day long did I cry unto him; yea, and when the night came I did still* **raise my voice** *high that it reached the heavens. And there came a voice unto me, saying: Enos, thy* **sins are forgiven thee,** *and thou shalt be blessed. And I, Enos, knew that God could not lie; wherefore, my* **guilt was swept away.** *And I said: Lord, how is it done? And he said unto me: Because of thy faith in Christ, whom thou hast never before heard nor seen and many years pass away before he shall manifest himself in the flesh; wherefore, go to,* **thy faith hath made thee whole."** (Enos 4-8)

Mormon teaches us of the importance of being found guiltless when he said, *"…And he hath brought to pass the redemption of the world, whereby he that is found* **guiltless** *before him at the judgment day hath it given unto him to* **dwell** *in the* **presence of God** *in his kingdom, to sing ceaseless praises with the choirs above, unto the Father, and unto the Son, and unto the Holy Ghost, which are one God, in a state of* **happiness** *which hath* **no end."** (Mormon 7:7)

If we are to be found guiltless, then we must fully repent of all our sins, while we are still in this life. For the Lord spoke through the prophet Amulek and said, *"Yea, I would that ye would come forth and harden not your hearts any longer; for behold, **now is the time and the day of your salvation**; and therefore, if ye will **repent** and harden not your hearts, immediately shall the great plan of redemption be brought about unto you. For behold, **this life is the time for men to prepare** to meet God; yea, behold the day of this life is the day for men to perform their labors. And now, as I said unto you before, as ye have had so many witnesses, therefore, I beseech of you that ye **do not procrastinate the day of your repentance** until the end; for after this day of life, which is given us to prepare for eternity, behold, if we do not improve our time while in this life, then cometh the night of darkness wherein there can be no labor performed. **Ye cannot say**, when ye are brought to that awful crisis that I will repent, that I will return to my God. Nay, ye cannot say this; for that same spirit which doth possess your bodies at the time that ye go out of this life, that **same spirit will have power to possess your body** in that eternal world. For behold, if ye have **procrastinated the day of your repentance** even until death, behold, ye have become subjected to the spirit of the devil, and he doth seal you his; therefore, the **Spirit of the Lord hath withdrawn from you**, and hath no place in you, and the devil hath all power over you; and this is the final state of the wicked. And this I know, because the Lord hath said **he dwelleth not in unholy temples**, but in the hearts of the righteous doth he dwell; yea, and he has also said that the righteous shall sit down in his kingdom, to go no more out; but their **garments should be made white through the blood of the Lamb."** (Alma 34:31-36)*

These truths are reiterated when Samuel the Lamanite said, *"But behold, your days of probation are past; ye have **procrastinated the day of your salvation** until it is everlastingly too late, and your destruction is made sure; yea, for ye have sought all the days of your lives for that which ye could not obtain; and ye have sought for happiness in doing iniquity, which thing is contrary to the nature of that righteousness which is in our great and Eternal Head. O ye people of the land, that ye would hear my words! And I pray that the anger of the Lord be turned away from you, and that ye would **repent and be saved."*** (Helaman 13:38-39)

In President Ezra Taft Bensons sermon, "Cleansing the Inner Vessel" he said, "*As I have sought direction from the Lord, I have had reaffirmed in my mind and heart the declaration of the Lord to* **'say nothing but repentance unto this generation'** (D&C 6:9; 11:9) *This is the theme of every latter-day prophet, along with their testimony that Jesus is the Christ and that Joseph Smith is a prophet of God….*

'*Thou shalt not be proud in thy heart,*' *the Lord warns us.* (D&C 43:40) '**Humble yourselves before God,**' *says the Book of Mormon.* (Mosiah 4:10) *When the* **earth is cleansed** *by burning in the last days, the* **proud shall be as stubble.** (see 3 Nephi 25:1: D&C 29:9; 64:24)…*Pride does not look up to God and care about what is right. It looks sideways to man and argues who is right.* **Pride is manifest in the spirit of contention. Was it not through pride that the devil became the devil?** *Christ wanted to serve. The devil wanted to rule. Christ wanted to bring men to where he was. The devil wanted to be above men. Christ removed self as the force in His perfect life. It was not my will, but thine be done. Pride is characterized by 'What do I want out of life?' rather than by 'What would God have me do with my life?'* **It is self-will as opposed to God's will.** *It is the fear of man over the fear of God.* **Humility responds to God's will**-*to the fear of His judgments and to the needs of those around us. To the proud, the applause of the world rings in their ears; to the humble, the applause of heaven warms their hearts. Someone has said, "Pride gets no pleasure out of having something, only out of having more of it than the next man." Of one brother, the Lord said, "I, the Lord, am not well pleased with him, for he seeketh to excel, and he is not sufficiently meek before me."* (D&C 58:41)… *With pride, there are many curses. With humility, there come many blessings. For example, "Be thou humble; and the Lord thy God shall lead thee by the hand, and give thee answer to thy prayers"* (D&C 122:10) *The humble will "be made strong, and blessed from on high, and receive knowledge."* (D&C 1:28) *The Lord is "***merciful** *unto those who* **confess their sins with humble hearts***"* (D&C 61:2) *Humility can turn away God's anger.* (See Helaman 11:11) *As we cleanse the inner vessel, there will have to be changes made in our own personal lives, in our families, and in the Church. The* **proud do not change** *to improve, but* **defend their position by rationalizing. Repentance means change,** *and it takes a humble person to change. But we can do it…*" ("A Witness and a Warning" p 73, 78-79.)

Often we hear the word repentance used in connection with serious sins, and of course, it is essential to teach the importance of repenting of our sins. Unfortunately, there are times when the true meaning of repentance is misunderstood. Because many people only associate repentance with grievous sin, they often think of repentance in a negative way. Comments such as "repentance is something you'll have to do, if you sin" or "repenting is something you don't want to have to do." Implies that repentance is so tough and painful that it is the consequence for sinning. Sin has many consequences such as; pain, guilt, and sorrow. However, repentance is not a consequence, it is the remedy, and the only way we can be cleansed from all sin, is to have all of our guilt swept away.

In the Bible Dictionary, **repentance** is defined with very inspired words, which you may want to look up, right now. The prophet Amulek also teaches this when he said, *"And I say unto you again that* **he cannot save them in their sins;** *for I cannot deny his word, and he hath said that* **no unclean thing can inherit the kingdom of heaven;** *therefore, how can ye be saved, except ye inherit the kingdom of heaven? Therefore,* **ye cannot be saved in your sins.**" (Alma 11:37).

In Alma 13:27-30, the prophet Alma pours out his feeling of great desire when he said, *"And now, my brethren, I wish from the inmost part of my heart, yea, with great anxiety even unto pain, that ye would hearken unto my words, and cast off your sins, and* **not procrastinate the day of your repentance.** *But that ye would* **humble** *yourselves before the Lord, and call on his holy name, and* **watch and pray continually,** *that ye may not be tempted above that which ye can bear, and thus be* **led by the Holy Spirit, becoming humble, meek, submissive, patient, full of love** *and* **all long-suffering;** *Having* **faith on the Lord;** *having a* **hope** *that ye* **shall receive eternal life;** *having the* **love of God always** *in your hearts, that ye may be lifted up at the last day and enter into his rest. And may the Lord grant* **unto you repentance,** *that ye may not bring down his wrath upon you, that ye may not be bound down by the chains of hell, that ye may* **not suffer the second death.**"

Elder Marion G. Romney stated that, *"Forgiveness is as wide as repentance. Every person will be* **forgiven for all the transgression of which he truly** *repents. If he repents of **all** his sins, he shall stand **spotless** before God because of the atonement of our Master and Savior Jesus Christ…Such is the gift of God's merciful plan of redemption."* (CR 1955 Oct: 124)

To fully partaker of God's merciful plan and to receive **all** that He has. We need to pray with **all** the energy of our hearts, we need to come to him in **all** humility, and confess **all** of our sins to Him, with a totally broken heart, and contrite spirit. We need to keep **all** of the commandments, and **always** remember Him, that we may **always** have His Spirit to be with us. We need to obey the promptings of the Holy Ghost, and endure well to the end. Only then may we someday receive **all** that the Father has.

The prophet Nephi tell us, *"For we labor diligently to write, to persuade our children, and also our brethren, to believe in Christ, and to be reconciled to God; for we know that it is by grace that we are saved, after **all** we can do."* (2 Nephi 25:23) The importance of repenting of **all** of our sins is beautifully expressed in the Hymn "Father in Heaven, We Do Believe" written by Elder Parley P. Pratt.

Father in Heav'n, we do believe
The promise thou hast made;
Thy word with meekness we receive,
Just as thy Saints have said.

We now **repent of all our sin**
And come with **broken heart,**
And to thy **covenant enter in**
And **choose the better part.**

O Lord, accept us while we pray,
And all our sins forgive,
**New life** impart to us this day.
And bid the sinners live.

Humbly we take the sacrament
In Jesus' blessed name;
Let us receive thru covenant
The Spirit's heav'nly flame. (the baptism of fire)

We will be buried in the stream
In Jesus' blessed name,
And rise, while light shall on us beam
**The Spirit's heav'nly flame.**

Baptize us with the Holy Ghost (spiritual rebirth)
And seal us as thine own.
That we may join the ransomed host
And with the Saints be one. (be with the sanctified, be united)
(words in parenthesis added)

To become sanctified, or spiritually born of God, and receive the blessed gift of having "all" of your guilt swept away, you must confess all of your sins, as Enos did, which took him all day and into the night. For each person the process, and the experience is personalized, we each have are own private language, our unique interpretations, and our level of spiritual maturity. As you come to the Lord, in the deeps of humility and begin confessing each sin, the Spirit will remind you of sins you have forgotten, you will be shown your weaknesses that you need to confess and forsake.

In Ether 12:27 we read, *"And if men come unto me **I will show unto them their weakness**. I give unto men weakness that they **may be humble**; and my **grace** is sufficient for all men that **humble** themselves before me; for if they humble themselves before me, and have **faith in me**, then will I make weak things become strong unto them."*

If you come to the Lord with a sincere desire to truly repent and ask Him to show you, your weaknesses (the things you need to repent of). One by one the Spirit will show you each transgression you have not fully repented of. It is only after you have confessed all of our sins with godly sorrow and forsaken them, can you be totally forgiven. In the Lord's own time, when the Spirit can justify you, then Christ's atoning blood will sanctify and cleanse you from all sin and you will be born of God, and receive "the mighty change of heart." For you will "have no more disposition to do evil, but to do good continually." Thus weak things shall become strong unto you!!! (Ether 12:27) and your guilt will be swept away!

# CHAPTER 8

# *"Except a Man be Born Again"*

What did Jesus mean when he said to Nicodemus, "*Verily, verily, I say unto thee,* **Except a man be born again, he cannot see the kingdom of God.** *Nicodemus saith unto him, How can a man be born when he is old? can he enter the second time into his mother's womb, and be born? Jesus answered, Verily, verily, I say unto thee, Except a man be born of water* **and of the Spirit,** *he cannot enter into the kingdom of God. That which is born of the flesh is flesh; and that which is born of the Spirit is spirit. Marvel not that I said unto thee,* **Ye must be born again.**" (John 3:3-6)

"*...For no unclean thing can dwell there, or dwell in his presence;*" Moses 6:57 and in 3 Nephi 27:19-20, "*And* **no unclean thing can enter into his kingdom;** *therefore nothing entereth into his rest save it be those who have* **washed their garments in my blood,** *because of their* **faith,** *and the* **repentance of all their sins,** *and their* **faithfulness unto the end.** *Now this is the commandment: Repent, all ye ends of the earth, and come unto me and be baptized in my name, that ye* **may** *be* **sanctified** *by the* **reception** *of the* **Holy Ghost,** *that ye* **may stand spotless** *before me at the last day.*"

The only way we can stand spotless before God, is if we have been born of the Spirit, and become spiritually born again. We can become sanctified only by the reception of the Holy Ghost. When we are confirmed we are instructed to receive the Holy Ghost. However, for the vast majority of members of the church, it is a long time before they become spiritually mature enough, to totally consecrate their lives to the Lord, and strive to live by every word that proceedeth from the mouth of God, and come to the

Lord with a broken heart and a contrite spirit and confess **all** of their sins to Him. So that the Spirit of the Holy Ghost may justify them, and then the Saviors precious atoning blood may sanctify them. (See Moses 6:60)

Elder George Q. Cannon in the 1899 Oct. conference pg. 50 said, *"We need to be born again, and have new hearts put in us. There is too much of the old leaven about us. **We are not born again as we should be.** Do you not believe that we should become new creatures in Christ Jesus, under the influence of the Gospel? All will say, yes, who understand the Gospel. You must be born again. You must have new desires, new hearts, so to speak, in you. But what do we see? We see men* (and women) *following the ways of the world just as much as though they made no pretensions to being Latter-day Saints. Hundreds of people who are called Latter-day Saints you could not distinguish from the world. They have the **same desires,** the **same feelings,** the **same aspirations,** the **same passions** as the **rest of the world.** Is this how God want us to be? No; **He wants us to have new hearts, new desires.** He wants us to be a **changed people** when we embrace His Gospel, and to be animated by **entirely new motives,** and have a **faith that will lay hold of the promises of God."***

Alma the younger, teaches us these same truths when he said, *"Now I say unto you that **ye must repent, and be born again;** for the Spirit saith if ye are **not born again ye cannot inherit the kingdom of heaven;** therefore come and be baptized unto **repentance,** that ye **may** be washed from your sins, that ye **may have faith** on the **Lamb of God,** who taketh away the sins of the world, who is mighty to save and to **cleanse from all unrighteousness."** (Alma 7:14)

In Mosiah 27:25 we read, *"And the Lord said unto me: marvel not that all mankind, yea, men and women, all nations, kindreds, tongues and people, must be born again; yea, **born of God, changed** from their **carnal** and **fallen state,** to a **state of righteousness, being redeemed of God, becoming his sons and daughters;** And thus they become **new creatures;** and unless they do this thy can in **nowise inherit the kingdom of God."***

Our beloved Savior taught us these words, *"And behold, I have given you the law and the commandments of my Father, that ye shall believe in me, and that* *ye shall **repent of your sins,** and **come unto me** with a **broken heart** and a **contrite spirit.** Behold, ye have the commandments before you, and the law is fulfilled. Therefore **come unto me and be ye saved;** for verily I say unto you, that except ye shall **keep my commandments,** which I have commanded you at this time, ye shall in **no case enter into the kingdom of heaven."** (3 Nephi 12:19-20)*

In Matthew 18:3-5, Jesus said, *"Verily I say unto you, except ye be **converted, and become as little children, ye shall not enter into the kingdom of heaven.** Whosoever therefore shall **humble himself** as this little child, the same is greatest in the kingdom of heaven. And whoso shall receive one such little child in my name **receiveth me."***

In Revelations 3:19-21 the Lord says to us, *"As many as I love, I rebuke and chasten: **be zealous** therefore, **and repent.** Behold, I stand at the door, and knock: if any man hear my voice, and open the door, **I will come in to him,** and I will sup with him, and he with me. To him that overcometh will I grant to sit with me in my throne, even as I also overcame, and am set down with my Father in his throne."*

In President Ezra Taft Benson's book "A Witness and a Warning" p. 61-62, *"When you choose to follow Christ, you choose to be changed. "No man," said President David O. McKay, "can sincerely resolve to apply to his daily life the teachings of Jesus of Nazareth without sensing a **change in his own nature.** The phrase **'born again' has a deeper significance** than many people attach to it. This **changed feeling may be indescribable, but it is real."*** (Conference Report, April 1962 p. 7.)

*Our Lord told Nicodemus that "except a man be born again, he cannot see the kingdom of God."* (John 3:3) *Of these words President Spencer W. Kimball said, "This is the simple total answer to the weightiest of all questions....**To gain eternal life there must be a rebirth, a transformation.***" (Conference Report, April 1958, p) *President McKay said that Christ called for **"an entire revolution"** of Nicodemus's "inner man." "His manner of thinking, feeling, and acting with reference to spiritual things would have to **undergo a fundamental and permanent change."***

*In addition to the physical ordinance of baptism and the laying on of hands,* **one must be spiritually born again to gain exaltation and eternal life.***(Conf. Report April 1960 p. 26.)*

The Prophet Joseph Smith said the following, *"Every man lives for himself. Adam was made to open the ways of the world, and for dressing the garden. Noah was born to save seed of everything, when the earth was washed of its wickedness by the flood; and the Son of God came into the world to redeem it from the fall. But except a man be born again, he cannot see the Kingdom of God. This eternal truth settles the question of all men's religion. A man may be saved, after the judgment, in the terrestrial kingdom, or in the telestial kingdom, but* **he can never see the celestial Kingdom of God, without being born of water and of the Spirit.** *He may receive a glory like the moon, or a star, but he can never come unto Mount Zion, and unto the city of the living God, the heavenly Jerusalem, and to an innumerable company of angels, to the general assembly and Church of the Firstborn, which are written in heaven, and to God the Judge of all, and to the spirits of just men made perfect, and to Jesus the Mediator of the new covenant,* **unless he becomes as a little child,** *and is* **taught by the Spirit of God.** *Wherefore, we again say search the revelations of God; study the prophecies and rejoice that God grants unto the world seers and prophets."* (Evening and Morning Star, August 22, 1832)

In the book "Stand Ye In Holy Places" by Pres. Harold B. Lee on p. 60, the Prophet Joseph Smith is quoted in the *Times and Seasons,* *"Various and conflicting are the opinions of man with regard to the gift of the Holy Ghost. Some people have been in the habit of calling every supernatural manifestation the effects of the spirit of God, whilst there are* **others that think** *[there] is* **no manifestation connected** *with it at all; and that it is* **nothing but a mere impulse of the mind,** *or an* **inward feeling, impression,** *or* **secret testimony** *or evidence which men possess, and that there is no such thing as an outward manifestation. It is not to be wondered at that men should be* **ignorant,** *in a great measure, of the principles of salvation, and more especially of the* **nature, office, power, influence, gifts and blessings of the Gift of the Holy Ghost;** *when we consider that the human family have been enveloped in gross darkness and ignorance for many centuries past without revelation or any just criterion to* *arrive at a knowledge of the things of God which can **only be known by the spirit of God**. Hence it not infrequently occurs that when the elders of this church preach to the inhabitants of the world, that if they obey the gospel they shall receive the gift of the Holy Ghost, that people expect to see some wonderful manifestation; some great display of power, or some extraordinary miracle performed; and it is often the case that young members in this church, for want of better information, carry along with them their old notions of things and sometimes fall into egregious errors. We believe that the Holy Ghost is imparted by the laying on of hands of those in authority, and that the gift of tongues, and also the gift of prophecy, are gifts of the spirit, and are obtained through that medium; but then to say that men always prophesied and spoke in tongues when they had the imposition of hands, would be to state that which is untrue, contrary to the practice of the apostles, and at variance to holy writ. For Paul says: "For to one is given the gift of healing, and again do all prophesy, do all speak with tongues, do all interpret?..."* (Times and Seasons 1:823.)

In the book "On The Way To Immortality And Eternal Life" p.5, by Elder J. Reuben Clark, we read, *"Yet, in the words of an ancient prophet, many men "are lifted up in the **pride** of their eyes, and have stumbled, because of the greatness of their stumbling block...they **put down the power** and **miracles of God**, and **preach up unto themselves** their **own wisdom** and their **own learning**." Paul declared to the Corinthians the truth about the proud men of the world: 'But the **natural man receiveth not the things of the Spirit of God:** for they are **foolishness** unto him: **neither can he know them,** because they are **spiritually discerned.'** 'For what man knoweth the things of a man, save the spirit of man which is in him? even so the **things of God knoweth no man, but the Spirit of God,'** and 'the Spirit of God dwelleth in you.'* (speaking to those who had been born of God) *Men must put pride of their learning and their achievement from their hearts. And why not? For how like a drop in the ocean is the knowledge of the wisest **compared with the fullness of the truth of the universe.** Men must humbly confess Jesus as the Christ, "for there is **none other name** under heaven given among men, whereby we must be **saved.**"*

President Brigham Young stated, *"I know nothing about faith in the Lord, without works corresponding therewith; they must go together, for without works you cannot prove that faith exists. We might cry out, until the day of our death that we love the Savior, but if we neglect to observe his sayings he would not believe us."* (JD, Apr. 18, 1874, 17:40)

On February 17, 1847, Brigham Young was laying ill at Winter Quarters, when the Prophet Joseph Smith appeared to him in a dream. Pres. Young related the following; *"Joseph stepped toward me and looking very earnestly, yet pleasantly, said, 'Tell the people to be humble and faithful, and be sure to keep the spirit of the Lord and it will lead them right. Be careful and **do not turn away the still small voice**; it will teach them what to do and where to go; it will yield the fruits of the kingdom. Tell the brethren to keep their hearts open to conviction, so that **when the Holy Ghost comes to them**, their hearts will be ready to receive it. They can tell the Spirit of the Lord from all other spirits; it will **whisper peace and joy** to their souls; it will **take malice, strife, and all evil from their hearts**, and their **whole desire will be to do good**, bring forth **righteousness** and **build up** the **Kingdom of God**. Tell the brethren if they will follow the Spirit of the Lord, they will go right. Be sure and tell the people to keep the Spirit of the Lord, and if they will, they will find themselves just as they were organized by our Father in Heaven, before they came into the world. Our Father in Heaven organized the human family, but they are all disorganized and in great confusion.' "Joseph then showed me the pattern, how they were in the beginning. This I cannot describe, but I saw it, and saw where the priesthood had been taken from the earth (and then restored) and how it must be joined together, so that there would be a perfect chain, from Father Adam to his latest posterity. Joseph again said, 'Tell the people to be sure and keep the Spirit of the Lord and follow it, and it will lead them just right."*
("Exodus to Greatness by Preston Nibley, p 329)

Three times in this dream, Joseph counseled the members of the church to get, keep and follow the Spirit of the Lord. In "A New Witness for the Articles of Faith" p. 284-85 Elder McConkie wrote, *"Thus it is that the **saints are born of Christ** because they have been born of the Spirit; they are alive in Christ because they enjoy the companionship of the Spirit, and they are members of his family because they are **clean as he is clean.** "and under this head ye are made free"—being Christ, they are **free from the bondage** of sin—"* and *there is no other head (other than Christ our Head) whereby ye can be made free." Only those who accept Christ and **receive the Spirit can free** themselves from the **sins of the world**. "There is no other name given whereby salvation cometh; therefore, I would that ye should take upon you the name of Christ, all you that have entered into the covenant with God that ye should be **obedient unto the end of your lives**.*" (Mosiah 5:7-8) "*Those who are born again not only live a **new life**, but they also have a new father. Their **new life is one of righteousness**, and their **new father is God**. They become the sons of God; or, more particularly, they become the sons and daughters of **Jesus Christ**. They bear, ever thereafter, the name of their new parent; that is, they take upon themselves the name of Christ and become Christians, not only in word but in very deed. They become by adoption the **offspring of Christ**, the children in his family, the members of his household which is the perfect household of perfect faith. And further: Having become the sons of God (Christ), they also become joint-heirs with him of the fulness of the glory of the Father, thus becoming by adoption the sons of God the Father.*"

Elder McConkie continues on p. 280 with, "*As a member of the Eternal Godhead, the Holy Ghost is an eternal being. As a gift from Deity to man, the gift of the Holy Ghost has been available everlastingly. It is an **essential** part of the plan of salvation on this and on all worlds. Unless and until men **enjoy the gift** of the **Holy Ghost**, they **do not receive the fullness of the everlasting gospel and hence are not heirs of the fulness of salvation**. As pertaining to this earth and its inhabitants, Adam received the Holy Ghost and was born again, thus setting the pattern for his seed forever. After his spiritual rebirth "He heard a voice out of heaven, saying: Thou art **baptized with fire**, and with the **Holy Ghost**. This is the record of the Father, and the Son, 'from henceforth and forever; and thou art after the order of him who was without beginning of days or end of years, from all eternity to all eternity. Behold, thou are one in me, a **son of God**; and thus **may** all become my sons.*" (Moses 6:66-68)

In Elder McConkie's book "The Promised Messiah" p. 351 he said, "*In setting forth that all men **must be born again to gain salvation**, we have seen that this means they must be "born of God, **changed** from their carnal and fallen state, to a **state** of righteousness, being **redeemed** of God, becoming his* *sons and daughters."* (Mosiah 27:25) *Whose sons and daughters do we become when we are born again? Who is our new Father? The answer is, Christ is our Father; we become his children by adoption; he makes us members of his family. Nowhere is this set forth better than in the words of King Benjamin to his Nephite subjects. "Because of the covenant ye have made," he said (and it is the same covenant all of us make in the waters of baptism), "ye shall be called the* **children of Christ,** *his sons, and his daughters; for behold, this day he hath* **spiritually begotten** *you; for ye say that your* **hearts are changed** *through faith on his name; therefore, ye are born of him and have become his sons and his daughters."* (Mosiah 5:7)

Do you remember the painting of Jesus standing at the door knocking? Could it be that the door the Lord stands at is the one to your heart? Open your heart and let "your" Savior, "your" Redeemer, "your" Jesus in. Let Him all the way into the center of your heart. Love Him with all of your heart, might, mind and strength. Let all of your thoughts be directed to the Lord; let the affections of your heart be placed upon the Lord forever. (See Alma 37:36) He knows all of the thoughts and the intents of your heart. (See Alma 18:32) Your Heavenly Parents and the Lord Jesus Christ love you so dearly it is as if you were their only child. Jesus loves you so personally He would have suffered and died for just you alone. He stands patiently waiting for you to let Him into your heart, **where** He can heal you, both physically and spiritually. Then you will have a mighty change of heart, be spiritually born of God and be truly converted?

# CHAPTER 9

# *"The Natural Man is an Enemy to God"*

What is the Lord's definition of "the natural man?" Is it someone who continually chooses evil, or is the natural man, everyone who has not yet been spiritually born of God?

Elder Bruce R. McConkie wrote the following in "A NEW WITNESS FOR THE ARTICLES OF FAITH", on p. 282, "*There is a natural birth, and there is a spiritual birth. The natural birth is to die as pertaining to premortal life, to leave the heavenly realms where all spirits dwell in the Divine Presence, and to begin a new life, a mortal life, a life here on earth. The **natural birth creates a natural man, and the natural man is an enemy to God**. In his fallen state he is carnal, sensual, and devilish by nature. Appetites and passions govern his life and he is alive—acutely so— to all that is evil and wicked in the world. The spiritual birth comes after the natural birth. It is to die as pertaining to worldliness and carnality and to become a new creature by the power of the Spirit. It is to begin a **new life**, a life in which **we bridle our passions** and **control our appetites, a life of righteousness, a spiritual life**. Whereas we were in a deep abyss of darkness, now we are alive in Christ and bask in the shining rays of his everlasting light. Such is the new birth, the second birth, the **birth into the household of Christ**.*"

Also in "A NEW WITNESS FOR THE ARTICLES OF FAITH" p. 288, "*The Lord commanded Adam to teach his children: "By reason of transgression cometh the fall, which fall bringeth death." That is, death and procreation entered the world with the fall. Both of them appertain to mortality, and Adam lived in a deathless state of immortality before the fall. "And inasmuch as ye were born into the world by water, and blood, and the spirit, which I have made, and so became of dust a living soul," the Lord continued, "even so ye* **must be born again** *into the kingdom of heaven, of water, and of the Spirit, and* **be cleansed by blood,** *even the blood of mine Only Begotten."*

In Elder McConkie's book "THE PROMISED MESSIAH" p. 227, *"From King Benjamin, as he quoted the words of an angel, we learn: Christ "cometh unto his own, that salvation might come unto the children of men, even through faith on his name….For* **salvation cometh to none…except it be through repentance and faith on the Lord Jesus Christ.**…*For the natural man is an enemy to God, and has been from the fall of Adam, and will be, forever and ever, unless he* **yields** *to the* **enticings of the Holy Spirit,** *and* **putteth off the natural man** *and* **becometh a saint** *through the* **atonement of Christ the Lord,** *and* **becometh as a child, submissive, meek, humble, patient, full of love,** *willing to* **submit to all** *things which the* **Lord** *seeth fit to inflict upon him, even as a* **child** *doth* **submit to his father."** (Mosiah 3:8-19.) *Again from King Benjamin: "The atonement… has been prepared from the foundation of the world, that thereby salvation might come to him that should put his* **trust in the Lord,** *and should be* **diligent in keeping his commandments,** *and continue in the* **faith even unto the end** *of his life."* (Mosiah 4:6.) *And so, if need be, we might continue until we fill volumes. Everywhere and always when inspired men speak or write of being redeemed from the spiritual fall, of gaining salvation in the presence of Gods and angels, their voice is one of* **faith, repentance, baptism,** *and of* **receiving the Holy Ghost,** *and of thereafter pressing* **forward** *with* **steadfastness** *and* **devotion conforming to every principle of eternal truth."**

In "THE PROMISED MESSIAH" p. 349 we read, *"Death entered the world by means of Adam's fall—death of two kinds, temporal and spiritual. Temporal death passes upon all men when they depart this mortal life. It is then that the eternal spirit steps out of its earthly tenement, to take up an abode in a realm where spirits are assigned, to await the day of their resurrection.* **Spiritual death passes upon all men when they become accountable for** *their sins. Being thus subject to sin they die spiritually; they die as pertaining to the things of the Spirit; they die as pertaining to the things of righteousness; they are cast out of the presence of God. It is of such men that the scriptures speak when they say that the natural man is an enemy to God and has become carnal, sensual, and devilish by nature. If a man "yields to the enticings of the Holy Spirit, and putteth off the natural man and becometh a saint through the atonement of Christ the Lord"* (Mosiah 3:19), **then he is born again. His spiritual death ceases.** *He becomes alive to the things of the Spirit; he returns to the presence of God because he* **receives** *the gift of the Holy Ghost; and he is* **alive to the things of righteousness.** *He crucifies the old man of sin, becomes a* **new creature** *of the Holy Ghost, and* **walks in a newness of life.** *This is what is meant by being born again."*

Elder Neal A. Maxwell expands our understanding of these truths, in his book, "Notwithstanding My Weakness" p. 73.

*"The seeming shutters on the windows of heaven are but the natural scales on our own eyes. Paul said it well: "But the natural man receiveth not the things of the Spirit of God: for they are foolishness unto him: neither can he know them, because they are spiritually discerned."* (1 Corinthians 2:14.)

*Therefore,* **only** *to the* **extent** *that we are* **willing** *to* **put off** *the* **natural man** *do we have* **any real hope at all of becoming saints.** *It is the putting off, of the putting off that is our real problem, however.*

*Letting go of the world requires not only* **deliberate disengagement** *from the ways of the* **world,** *but also being willing to take the next step by* **yielding** *to the* **enticings** *of the* **Spirit.** *If one refuses to do both things, the prognosis is poor, for our childish rebellion will continue. "But remember that he that* **persists** *in his own* **carnal nature,** *and goes on in the ways of* **sin** *and* **rebellion against God, remaineth** *in his* **fallen state** *and the* **devil** *hath all* **power over him.** *Therefore, he is as though there was* **no redemption made,** *being an* **enemy to God; and also is the* **devil an enemy to God."** (Mosiah 16:5.)

*So far as our real self-interests are concerned,* **sin is irrational** *even when measured merely in the dimension of time. It is insanity when viewed by the* *eyes of eternity. Of course, the adversary's trick is to make that which* **hurts us** **seem pleasing** *and that which is* **ugly seem attractive.** *Such huckstering requires real cleverness—but, most of all, credulous consumers. Discerning consumerism is currently much urged in the marketplace of goods, but it is regarded as out of place in the bazaar of behavior!*

*If, however, one can begin to understand his position in this world and his relationship to our Heavenly Father, even though he may have previously spent much time as a patron in "Vanity Fair," it is not too late, as the earlier-quoted words of Malcolm Muggeridge attest.*

*When we begin to* **put off the natural man** *and move, however slightly, toward sainthood, we will find ourselves almost at once beginning to be stretched conceptually. It becomes possible for us to* **know things** *we did not believe it possible to know. "And now behold, my brethren, what* **natural man** *is there that* **knoweth these things?** *I say unto you, there is* **none that knoweth** *these things,* **save** *it be the* **penitent.***" (Alma 26:21.)

*We thus become eligible to receive "the things of the Spirit of God" which the* **natural man cannot receive.** (See 1 Corinthians 2:14.)

*The greater our yielding to the enticings of the Spirit, the more we are stretched conceptually and experientially. This was the case with Moses, who was highly developed spiritually. Being shown by God His creations, Moses declared that he had been shown things which he* **"never had supposed."** (Moses 1:10.) *When Moses observed after this marvelous experience that "man is nothing," this surely was not a reflection on man, "God's greatest miracle," but a placing of man in the vast perspective of God's creations and a realizing, even so, that* **we** *are* **God's exclusive work** *and his* **greatest glory.** *What a marvelous rejoinder Moses' vision is to those who superficially seize upon adjectives like carnal, sensual, and devilish* **as a means of excusing themselves** *from any effort to be otherwise!*

*Only to the extent that we put off the natural man can we eventually* **abide the** **presence of God** *and see Him.* (See D&C 67:10-12.) *Likewise,* **only** *when we* **put off** the **natural man** and become **saints** can we **then** have **access** to the **powers of heaven** and handle them **properly.** No longer would we then use power and authority to "cover our sins" or to "gratify our pride, or our vain ambition." **No longer** would we "exercise control or dominion or compulsion upon the souls of the children of men, in **any** degree of unrighteousness. "(D&C 121:3.) Who would care to tally the misery in human history resulting from the unrighteous use of power, whether in peer pressures or dictatorships? Rather, having so qualified by **responding** to the **"enticings of the Spirit"** we would find that "the Holy Ghost shall be thy **constant companion,** and thy scepter an unchanging scepter of **righteousness** and **truth;** and thy dominion shall be an everlasting dominion, and **without compulsory means** it shall flow unto thee forever and ever." (D&C 121:46. Italics added.) *Only as we become* **partakers** *of the* **divine nature** *are we* **qualified** *to become* **partakers** *of* **divine power.**

Furthermore, as we progress in this manner spiritually, we will not only **confess** God's hands in all things and do so **gladly,** but we will also be able to connect correct concepts and to see how **all** His commandments are **spiritual.** (See D&C 29:35.)

**Saintlike individuals seem to be so rare** that we have almost ceased thinking about what living in a society of saints would be like. Such a people existed for several decades. There was **real** peace, **real** freedom, **prosperity without poverty,** an **absence** of envy, lying, violence, whoredoms, and lasciviousness; "surely there could not be a **happier** people." (4 Nephi 1:16.)
Some may freely say that they do not wish to meet the terms set down by God for achieving such ideal conditions. But given the fact that God is there and these are His terms, we are not able to reorder these realities of the universe to multiply the options. **Our choice** is to **seek** to **establish His righteousness** or to **rebelliously** continue to walk in our **own way.**

We are free to choose, to obey or not to obey, to come to terms or not to come to terms with the Lord. But **we cannot revise** the **terms.** And even the refusal to come to terms with God will, ere long, be an option no longer open, for every knee will bow and every tongue will confess that **Jesus is the Christ.** Even those who have lived without God in the world will finally confess that God has **dealt justly** with them. (See Mosiah 16:1.)

*Once we have come to terms, however, then come the **steps toward sainthood**. And mere steps they are, as we learn to become **submissive, humble, meek, patient,** and **full of love.*** (Mosiah 3:19.)

*This process of putting off and becoming, however, requires the **constant light** of the gospel so that we can see and understand what we are doing."*

The entire verses of Mosiah 3:19-21 reads, *"For the natural man is an enemy to God, and has been from the fall of Adam, and will be, forever and ever, **unless** he yields to the enticings of the Holy Spirit, and putteth off the natural man and becometh a **saint** through the atonement of Christ the Lord, and becometh as a child submissive, meek, humble, patient, full of love, willing to submit to all things which the Lord seeth fit to inflict upon him, even as a child doth submit to his father." And moreover, I say unto you, that the time shall come when the knowledge of a Savior shall spread throughout every nation, kindred, tongue, and people. And behold, when that time cometh, **none shall be found blameless before God,** except it be little children, **only through repentance** and **faith** on the **name** of the **Lord God Omnipotent."***

In "GOSPEL TRUTH", p. 293 by Elder George Q. Cannon we read, *"In the prayer of the brother of Jared to the Lord…the Prophet used this language: "**Because** of the **fall** our **natures** have become **evil continually;** nevertheless, O Lord, thou hast given us a commandment that we must call upon thee, that from thee we may **receive according** to our **desires.***" (Ether 3:2.)

*The fall that was here referred to by the brother of Jared took place when Adam and Eve disobeyed the command of God and partook of the forbidden fruit and were driven out of Eden. Through that act the natures of man and his posterity became, as the Prophet said, **subject to evil continually….***

*The Gospel has been revealed to save man from all the consequences of the fall…While **here** in this probation, we have to struggle to **overcome our fallen natures** and to bring them in subjection to the holy principles which we call the Gospel of Jesus Christ. It requires a constant struggle for all human beings to resist the temptations of Satan who appeals to us and tries to obtain power over us through **our fallen natures.***" (May 15, 1900, JI 35:312)

The brother of Jared acknowledges our fallen nature, when he prayed, *"O Lord, thou hast said that we must be encompassed by the floods. Now behold, O Lord, and do not be angry with thy servant because of his weakness before thee; for we know that thou are holy and dwellest in the heavens, and that we are **unworthy before thee; because** of the **fall** our **natures** have become **evil continually**; nevertheless, O Lord, thou hast given us a commandment that we must call upon thee, that from thee we may receive according to our desires."*
Ether 3:2

In Alma 42:9-26, we read how only the truly penitent are saved from all of the effects of the fall. *"Therefore, as the soul could never die, and the fall had brought upon **all** mankind a **spiritual death as well as a temporal**; that is, they were cut off from the presence of the Lord; it was expedient that mankind should be **reclaimed** from this spiritual death; therefore, as they had become carnal, sensual, and devilish by nature, this probationary state became a **state for them to prepare**; it became a preparatory state. And now remember, my son, if it were not for the plan of redemption, (laying it aside,) as soon as they were dead, their souls were miserable, being cut off from the presence of the Lord. And now there was no means to reclaim men from this fallen state which man had brought upon himself, because of his own disobedience; therefore, according to justice, the plan of redemption could not be brought about, **only on conditions of repentance of men in this probationary state**; yea, this preparatory state; for except it were for these conditions, mercy could not take effect except it should destroy the work of justice. Now the work of justice could not be destroyed; if so, God would cease to be God. And thus we see that **all mankind were fallen**, and they were in the grasp of justice; yea, the justice of God, which consigned them forever to be cut off from his presence. And now the **plan of mercy** could not be brought about, except an **atonement** should be made; therefore God himself atoneth for the sins of the world, to bring about the plan of mercy, to appease the demands of justice, that God might be a **perfect, just God,** and a **merciful God** also. Now **repentance** could not come unto men, except there were a **punishment**, which also was eternal as the life of the soul should be, affixed opposite to the plan of happiness, which was as eternal also as the life of the soul. Now, how could a man repent, except he should sin? How could he sin, if there was no law? How could there be a law, save there was a punishment? Now there was a **punishment affixed**, and a just law* *given, which brought **remorse** of conscience unto man. Now if there was no law given if a man murdered he should die, would he be afraid he would die if he should murder? And also, if there was no law given against sin, men would not be afraid to sin. And if there was no law given if men sinned, what could justice do, or mercy either; for they would have no claim upon the creature? But there is a **law given,** and a **punishment affixed,** and a **repentance granted;** which **repentance, mercy claimeth;** otherwise, justice claimeth the creature, and executeth the law, and the law inflicteth the punishment: if not so, the works of justice would be destroyed, and God would cease to be God. But God ceaseth not to be God, and **mercy claimeth the penitent,** and mercy cometh because of the **atonement;** and the atonement bringeth to pass the resurrection of the dead; and the resurrection of the dead bringeth back men into the presence of God; and thus they are restored into **his presence,** to be judged according to their works; according to the law and justice; for behold, **justice exerciseth all his demands.** and also **mercy claimeth all which is her own;** and thus, **none but the truly penitent are saved.** What! do ye suppose that **mercy can rob justice?** I say unto you, nay; **not one whit.** If so, God would cease to be God. And thus God bringeth about his great and eternal purposes, which were prepared from the foundation of the world. And thus cometh about the **salvation and the redemption of men,** and also their destruction and **misery.**"*

In Mosiah 3:11-13, we are taught, "*For behold, and also **his** blood atoneth for the sins of those who have **fallen** by the **transgression** of **Adam,** who have died not knowing the will of God concerning them, or who have ignorantly sinned. **But wo, wo unto him who knoweth that he rebelleth against God!** For salvation cometh to none such except it be through **repentance** and **faith on the Lord Jesus** Christ. And the Lord God hath sent his holy prophets among all the children of men, to declare these things to every kindred, nation, and tongue, that thereby whosoever should believe that Christ should come, the same **might** receive **remission of their sins,** and rejoice with **exceedingly great joy,** even as though he had already come among them.*

Next let us turn to Mosiah 16:5 & 12, 13, "*But remember that he that persists in his own carnal nature, and goes on in the ways of sin and rebellion against God, **remaineth in his fallen state** and the devil hath all power over him.*

*Therefore he is as though there was **no redemption** made, being an enemy to God; and also is the devil an enemy to God…Having gone according to their own carnal wills and desires; having never called upon the Lord while the arms of mercy were extended towards them; for the arms of mercy were extended towards them, and they would not; they being **warned of their iniquities** and yet they would not depart from them; and they were **commanded to repent** and yet they would not repent. And now, ought ye not to **tremble** and **repent of your sins**, and remember that only in and through Christ ye can be saved?*

Our contemporary definitions, of terms such as sin, wickedness, iniquities and even repentance, are often the natural man's definitions. And since the natural man is an enemy to God, these words often lose much of their true meaning. They are watered down to justify the natural man's thoughts and deeds. However, the Lord delights in plainness, and truth. Only when we remember that God can not look upon sin with the least degree of allowance, and that no unclean thing can dwell in the presence of God, and that we will be judged according to our thoughts, words, and deeds, do we begin to understand the Lord's definition of sin, wickedness and the fallen state of man. Only then do we begin to realize that everyone must fully repent, confess all of our sins to God, truly give away all of our sins that we may know Him. "*…and be reconciled to God; for we know that it is by grace that we are saved, after all we can do.*" (2 Nephi 25:23)

We must put off the natural man and become true saints, for "*neither can any natural man abide the presence of God,*" (D&C 67:12) We must be cleansed from all sin and be spiritually born of God, if we are to inherit the celestial kingdom. For the Lord said… "*Except a man be born again, he cannot see the kingdom of God.*" (John 3:3). And in Moses 6:59 we read, "*That by reason of transgression cometh the fall, which fall bringeth death, and inasmuch as ye were born into the world by water, and blood, and the spirit, which I have made, and so become of dust a living soul, even so ye **must be born again into the kingdom of heaven**, of water, and of the Spirit, and be cleansed by blood, even the blood of mine Only Begotten; that ye **might be sanctified from all sin**, and **enjoy the words of eternal life in this world**, and **eternal life** in the world to come even immortal glory.*"

Pres. Joseph F. Smith wrote, "*Of what use is it that we know the truth, if we lack its spirit? Our knowledge, in this event, becomes a condemnation to us, failing to bear fruit. It is not sufficient that we know the truth, but we must be humble and with this knowledge possess the spirit to actuate us to good deeds. Baptism, as well as all other outward ordinances, without the spirit accompanying, is useless. We remain but baptized sinners. It is the duty of the young men* (and all members) *of Israel to seek first the Kingdom of God and his righteousness, and leave other things to follow; to seek the spirit of truth so as to possess the knowledge of God, which giveth them a desire for purity, light, truth; and a spirit to despise evil and to turn away from all that is not of God.*" TLDP 284-285 (parenthesis added)

In more recent years, Elder Joseph Fielding Smith said, "*The Holy Ghost will not dwell in unclean tabernacles or disobedient tabernacles. The Holy Ghost will not dwell with that person who is unwilling to obey and keep the commandments of God or who violates those commandments willingly. In such a soul the spirit of the Holy Ghost cannot enter. That great gift comes to us only through humility and faith and obedience. Therefore, a great many members of the Church do not have that guidance.*" TLDP 279

You may be thinking that these things are hard to bear. Do you remember what Nephi said to his brothers, "*…I said unto them that I knew that I had spoken hard things against the wicked,* (natural man) *according to the truth; and the righteous have I justified, and testified that they should be lifted up at the last day; wherefore, the guilty taketh the truth to be hard, for it cutteth them to the very center.*" 1 Nephi 16:2 (words in parenthesis added)

We must put off the natural man and replace the thoughts of the world, with thoughts of our Lord Jesus Christ. If we direct our thoughts to the Lord continually, we will become more and more like Him. "*For as a man thinketh in his heart so is he.*" In order to become like our Savior, we must love Him with all of our hearts. For "*No man can serve two masters: for either he will hate the one and love the other; or else he will hold to the one, and despise the other. Ye cannot serve God and mammon.*" Matt 6:24 (the footnotes refer to mammon as idolatry, treasures and worldliness)

If worldly things occupy our thoughts constantly, who do we really serve and love? If we truly love the Lord with all of our hearts, might, minds and strength, we will strive to direct our thoughts to Him continually. (See Alma 73:36, D&C 6:36)

Do you remember when you where deeply in love? How many times a day did you think of your loved one? What were the feelings of your heart? The Lord Jesus Christ loves you very personally, with perfect celestial love. He loves you more dearly than any mortal ever could. He knows all of the thoughts and the intents of your heart. (See D&C 6:16, 33:1) and he longs for each of us to come unto Him, and fervently love Him with all our hearts. So that He can heal us and save us from our sins.

The process of coming unto Christ, also requires integrity with yourself. It takes a great deal of courage to look honestly into your own heart, and without any rationalizing or justifying, uncover the real you, to yourself. Many people are afraid to look deeply inside because they believe "The Big Lie," that their real self is defective and unrepairable and that they are really unlovable and incapable of becoming Christ-like.

These false beliefs begin in early childhood, when a child is told everything to say, feel, think, and do. The child either comes to believe that he can't do anything right, so he doesn't dare choose for himself, or he is provoked into anger, because his agency isn't honored, and then he is shamed for being angry. He is conditioned into believing that he is bad, stupid, and rebellious. Unfortunately, even the most caring parents unknowingly resort to brainwashing techniques, at times, by using force mode methods; such as physical punishment, yelling, scolding, threatening, blaming, shaming, and name calling. And when sleeping and eating times are unscheduled, it causes a great deal of stress, and irritability to babies, preschoolers, and older children. These choice celestial angels are very sensitive, and can experience a great deal of trauma when parents follow Satan's plan of force. All of this is done with the justification that "you have to force them to be obedient, respectful children."

Since when did Satan's plan ever help anyone become more obedient and respectful? When the Adversary's plan of force is used, the trusting child believes everything adults say, so he believes that he is bad, unworthy, incapable, unloved, the cause of all the contention, that he'll never be good enough, and that he has to do everything perfect to be loved. If his hurt feelings don't seem to matter to anyone, then he believes that he must not matter. These negative sub-conscience beliefs ARE LIES.

Can you see why Satan's plan could never work, because it is using brainwashing strategies. It is in direct conflict with the Lord's laws of love, persuasion, long-suffering, gentleness, meekness, kindness, pure knowledge without hypocrisy and without guile. (See D&C 121:41-42) The young child, (who was nurtured in celestial love for eons of time) naturally wants to be obedient, when Heavenly Father's honoring plan is used.

The true spirit self is always very loveable and capable. It is only by shining the spotlight of truth on a lie that we are able to see that these negative thoughts are false. Each time a negative, low self-worth thought enters your mind, place the flashlight of truth on it, by telling yourself; "My Heavenly Parents and Jesus love me as dearly as if I were their only Child. I am loveable and capable, because I am a Child of God." The instant truth shines on a lie it vanishes, and the darkness flees. The more often you fill your mind with the light of truth, the more quickly you will rediscover the marvelous truth of who you have always been for eons of time, a magnificent, unique, loveable, capable, divine being, worthy of being born again!!!

In addition to keeping a prayer in your heart more continually, you may want to write down some positive thoughts, and say them over and over whenever you have a few moments during the day. This will help fill your mind with truth and the truth will make you free! Free from the lies that you're not good enough; free from the fears that may be keeping you from truly coming to the Lord; free from the fears and lies that are lessening your faith; free from the belief that you are a human doing instead of a human being; and free from the lies that your worth is based upon your performance and your possessions.

You are of infinite worth because you are God's Child, PERIOD! When the Lord said: "be ye therefore perfect," He is inviting us to come and be perfected in Him. It is an invitation of love and to have faith in his atoning sacrifice. He didn't say be ye therefore a perfectionist, which is fear based and filled with the lie that your salvation is determined by how much you do, instead of rediscovering who you really are, and coming to Christ.

Are you honest with yourself? Are you becoming more teachable, humble, and penitent? Are you becoming more selfless, kind, patient, tolerant, and forgiving, even forgiving those who may never apologize to you in this life.

If you set aside an hour to imagine, **in detail,** the apology the offenders will give you in the next life, when they have a perfect remembrance of all their guilt and will feel the pain they have caused you. Then in tears, they beg you to forgive them, it will help you to forgive them totally, as you ask the Lord for the gift of forgiveness. This is an essential part of being totally forgiven of all of your sins.

Self-introspection will assist you in seeing what the Lord wants you to change. So in the spirit of love, may I ask you a few questions? Do you spend several hours each day, viewing (and in a sense worshiping) the things that are made by the hands of men? (such as the TV, computer, etc.) Do you try to fill up the feelings of emptiness with the things of this world? Do you try to comfort yourself with addictions, instead of seeking for the Holy Spirit to be your comforter? Do you spend more hours than are necessary, for your daily bread, seeking the treasures of the world, which moth and dust doth corrupt? Do you have your thoughts directed continually upon the things of the world, or upon the Lord? Do you truly love the Lord with all our hearts, might, mind and strength, or do the images of the world monopolize your thoughts?

Remember "*as a man thinketh in his heart so is he* "and "*where your treasure is there will your heart be also.*" (Matt 6:21)

My purpose in asking you these questions is not to start you on a guilt trip, because typically, guilt trips are non-productive expeditions that lead into the dark roads of despair, discouragement, and even self-hate. The Lord loves the sinner, not the sin. He separates us from our mistakes. Shouldn't we do the same, by admitting "I made a mistake, I make lots of mistakes, but I am not a mistake. I am a child of God of infinite worth, with the capability of becoming like Him!!!"

In order to put off the natural man, and become a true saint, believe Christ, believe in the atonement, and believe that if you faithfully strive to keep all of the commandments, obey the promptings of the Holy Spirit, and diligently seek Him, you will find Him. Come to the Lord, in godly sorrow, and confess all of your sins to Him. Turn your life over to the Lord and in all the sincerity of your heart saying, "not my will but thine be done." Live righteously, so that the Spirit may justify you. Then and only when it is according to God's timing, will Christ's precious blood sanctify you, and cleanse you from all sin. You will feel all of your guilt swept away; you will be filled with exceeding great joy, having been spiritually born of God; having put off the natural man, and become a true saint.

CHAPTER 10

# *"Humbled my Soul with Fasting; and Prayer"*

Fasting is also an essential step in becoming sanctified. Because it humbles our souls, strengthens our spirituality and our self-mastery. In Psalms 34:13 we read, "*…I **humbled my soul with fasting**; and my prayer returned into mine own bosom.*" and in Psalms 69:10, "*When I wept, and **chastened** my soul with fasting, that was to my reproach.*" It is only with a humble, broken heart and contrite spirit that we can offer up an acceptable sacrifice, when we confess our sins to the Lord. All those who truly come to the Lord, humble their souls by praying with all the energy and sincerity of their hearts and by fasting often.

In the book "PRAYER, on p. 101,102, Elder Robert L. Simpson wrote, "*There are no better examples of teaching by the Spirit than the sons of Mosiah. The Book of Mormon tells us how they became "strong in the knowledge of the truth; for they were men of a sound understanding and they had **searched the scriptures diligently**, that they might know the word of God. "But this is not all; they had given themselves to **much prayer, and fasting**; therefore they had the spirit of **prophecy**, and the spirit of **revelation**, and when they taught, they taught with power and authority of God.*" (Alma 17:2-3.)

*Is there a priesthood or auxiliary leader any place in this church who wouldn't give all to possess such power, such assurance? **Remember this above all else**, that according to Alma, they gave themselves to much **fasting and prayer**. You see, there are certain blessings that can only be fulfilled as we conform to* *a particular law. The Lord made this very clear through the Prophet Joseph Smith when he declared: "For all who will have a **blessing** at my hands shall **abide** the **law which was appointed for that blessing**, and the conditions thereof, as were instituted from before the foundation of the world." (D&C 132:5) Now, the Lord could not have stated the position more clearly, and, in my opinion, too many Latter-day Saint parents today are depriving themselves and their children of one of the **sweetest spiritual experiences** that the Father has made available to them.*

*When fasting…" we reap a particular spiritual benefit that can come to us in no other way. It is a **sanctification of the soul** for us today just as it was for some choice people who lived two thousand years ago: "Nevertheless they did **fast** and **pray oft**, and did wax stronger and **stronger in their humility**, and firmer and **firmer** in the **faith of Christ**, unto the filling their **souls with joy and consolation,** yea, even to the **purifying** and the **sanctification** of their hearts, which **sanctification cometh because** of their **yielding their hearts unto God.**"* (Helaman 3:35.) *Wouldn't you like this to happen to you? **It can, you know!***

*Did you notice the scripture says that those who do this have their souls **filled with** "**joy** and **consolation?**" You see, the world in general thinks that fasting is a time for "sackcloth and ashes," a time to carry a look of sorrow, as one to be pitied. On the contrary, the Lord admonishes: "Moreover when ye fast, be not, as the hypocrites, of a sad countenance: for they disfigure their faces that they may appear unto men to fast. Verily I say unto you, they have their reward.*

*"But thou, when thou fastest, anoint thine head, and wash thy face; "That thou appear not unto men to fast, but unto thy Father which is **in secret**: and thy Father, which seeth in secret, shall **reward thee openly.**"* (Matthew 6:16-18.)

In "A NEW WITNESS FOR THE ARTICLES OF FAITH, p. 302 Elder McConkie states, *"For verily this [my holy day] is a day appointed unto you to rest from your labors, and to pay thy devotions unto the Most High." Cease from servile work on the Sabbath; rest as pertaining to temporal pursuits; do the Lord's work on the Lord's day. Worship the Lord. "Nevertheless thy vows shall be offered up in **righteousness** on all days and **at all times.**" True wor-*

*ship goes on seven days a week. Sacraments and vows and covenants of renewal ascend to heaven daily in personal prayer. "But remember that on this, the Lord's day, thou shalt offer thine oblations and thy sacraments unto the Most High, **confessing thy sins** unto thy brethren, and before the Lord." Our oblations are our offerings to the Lord; they are both temporal and spiritual. We pay our fast offerings and make our means available for the furtherance of the Lord's work on earth. Such offerings are temporal. But we also offer to the Lord a **broken heart** and a **contrite spirit.** These offerings are **spiritual,** and when we make them, it is accounted unto us as though we had put all things on the altar.*

*"On this day thou shalt do none other thing, only let thy food be prepared with singleness of heart that thy **fasting may be perfect,** or, in other words, that they **joy may be full.** Verily, this is fasting and prayer, or in other words, rejoicing and prayer."* (D&C 59:10-14) *Rejoice in the Lord on his holy day! **Fast; pray; worship. Pay thy devotions!** It is the Lord's day; do thereon the things he wants done…"*

In Alma 17:9, *"…they **fasted much** and **prayed much** that the Lord would grant unto them a portion of **his Spirit** to go with them, and **abide** with them, that they might be and instrument in the hands of God…"*

In Isaiah 58:1-2, 6-8 we read, *"Cry aloud, spare not, lift up thy voice like a trumpet, and shew my people their **transgression**, and the house of Jacob their **sins**. Yet they seek me daily, and delight to know my ways, as a nation that did righteousness, and forsook not the **ordinance of their God:*** (keeping temple covenants*) they ask of me the ordinances of justice; they take delight in approaching to God….Is not this the **fast that I have chosen?** (*having a righteous attitude towards fasting*) to **loose** the **bands of wickedness**, to undo the heavy burdens, and to let the oppressed go free,*(free from the bondage of sin, and addictions) *and that ye break every yoke? Is it not to deal thy bread to the hungry, and that thou bring the poor that are cast out to thy house? When thou seest the naked, that thou cover him; and that thou hide not thyself from thine own flesh?* (those who will not help their own family) *Then shall thy light break forth as the morning, and thine health shall spring forth speedily: and **thy righteousness shall go before thee; the glory of the Lord shall be thy reward."***

In Joel 2:12 we read, *"Therefore also now, saith the Lord, turn ye even to me with **all your heart**, and with **fasting**, and with **weeping**, and with **mourning**:* (godly sorrow) *And **rend your heart**,* (a broken heart) *and not your garments, and turn unto the Lord your God: for he is gracious and merciful, slow to anger, and of great kindness, and repenteth him of the evil."* (parenthesis added)

In "Doctrine and Covenants Commentary" p. 352-353 Elder Bruce R. McConkie stated that, *"Fasting, as an expression of sorrow, is natural, for in deep affliction man does not crave nourishment to the same extent as under normal conditions. In the Law of Moses one annual fast day was provided—the day of atonement (Lev. 23:27-29). But on solemn occasions other fast days were observed. Joshua and the leading Elders of Israel were prostrate before the Ark one entire day after the defeat in the battle of Ai (Jos. 7:6). David fasted when his child was sick (II. Sam. 12:16). Moses fasted forty days on Mount Horeb. Elijah fasted a similar period, as did our Lord before entering upon His ministry. The children of God, in all ages, have found **comfort and strength in fasting** and **prayer**. In **answer to prayer** with fasting, extending over a period of two days and nights, Alma was healed. (Mosiah 27:22,23) Alma fasted and prayed many days, in order to **receive a testimony** of the truth. (Alma 5:46) There are many instances of fasting recorded in the Book of Mormon. Paul reminded the Saints that he and his companions had proved themselves to be ministers of God in "fasting" as well as in all other circumstances (II. Cor. 6:5). Our Lord warns His disciples **not to fast as hypocrites** who look sad and distort their countenances, in order to be seen by men, but to appear as if going to a social function, in order that God, "who seeth in secret" may reward them openly (Matt. 6:16-18). This is in harmony with what God revealed through Joseph the Prophet, that fasting should be **rejoicing**. It is also in harmony with the view taken by Isaiah (58:3-8). The Latter-day Saints have a Fast Sunday every month, on which they bear testimony to the goodness of the Lord to them, and remember the poor by donations. **If they understand the gospel, they will make every Sunday a fast-Sunday,** by abstaining from work, partaking of simple food, and devoting the day to spiritual matters.*
*15. And inasmuch as ye do these things with thanksgiving, with cheerful hearts and countenances, not with much laughter, for this is sin, but with a glad heart and a cheerful countenance—*

*16. Verily I say, that inasmuch as ye do this, the fulness of the earth is yours, the beasts of the field and the fowls of the air, and that which climbeth upon the trees and walketh upon the earth;* (D&C 59:14-16)

In the book "Evidences And Reconciliations" by Elder John A. Widtsoe, he states, "*That is, on the Sabbath day every person shall (1)* **attend** *meetings, (2)* **fast, if desired***, and always if it is a regular fast day, (3)* **partake** *of the sacrament, (4)* **bear testimony** *of the Lord's truth and goodness, (5)* **make right** *any misunderstandings with his fellow men, and (6) do all things with a "***single-ness of heart,***" toward the divine purpose of the Sabbath day. If these things be done in the proper spirit, the* **Sabbath** *becomes a day of "***rejoicing and prayer.***" And it should be noted that the commandment is for* **all** *members of the Church.*"

President David O. McKay said, "*All the principles related to fasting seem to point to the fact that it produces (1) physical benefits; (2) intellectual activity: and (3)* **spiritual strength,** *which is the* **greatest of all benefits***. This fine spiritual strength is derived by the subjection of the physical appetite to the will of the individual…If there were no other virtue in fasting but* **gaining strength of character** *that alone would be sufficient justification for its universal acceptance.*" TLDP: 199

President Joseph F. Smith stated, "*It is evident that the acceptable fast is that which carries with it the* **true spirit of love for God** *and* **man***; and the aim in fasting is to secure* **perfect purity of heart** *and* **simplicity of intention***-a fasting unto God in the fullest and* **deepest sense-for such a fast** *would be a* **cure** *for every practical and intellectual error; vanity would disappear, love for our fellows would take its place, and we would gladly assist the poor and the needy.*" (TLDP: 199)

President Joseph F. Smith also said, "*Observing the law of the fast would call attention to the sin of overeating, place the* **body in subjection to the spirit,** *and so promote* **communion** *with the Holy Ghost, and insure a* **spiritual strength** *and power which the people of the nation so greatly need.*" (*Gospel Doctrine p 237-238*)

Elder John A. Widtsoe stated, "*The Church urges all to observe the monthly fasts, and advises that **fasts at other times be engaged in wisely**, with due respect to the conditions and needs of the body.*" (PCG p.377)

In October conference 1974, p. 92, President Ezra Taft Benson said that, "*Periodic fasting can help clear up the mind and strengthen the body and the spirit. The usual fast, the one we are asked to participate in for fast Sunday, is for **24 hours** without food or drink. Some people feeling the need, have gone on longer fasts of abstaining from food but have taken the needed liquids. **Wisdom** should be used, and the fast should be broken with **light eating**. To make a fast most fruitful, it should be coupled with **prayer and meditation**; physical work should be held to a minimum, and it's a blessing if one can **ponder** on the scriptures and the reason for the fast.*"

Elder Delbert L. Stapley, in the October conference of 1951 p. 122- 123 said, "*The Saints by fasting and praying can **sanctify the soul** and elevate the spirit to **Christ like perfection**, and thus the body would be brought into **subjection** to the spirit, promote **communion with the Holy Ghost**, and **insure spiritual strength** and **power** to the individual. By observing fasting and prayer in its **true spirit**, the Latter-day Saints **cannot be overpowered** by Satan tempting them to evil.*"

# "Pray Always"

Prayer is absolutely an essential part of proper fasting. The remainder of this chapter will focus on the importance of fervent, sincere prayer and what it means to pray always.

"*Yea, he that **repenteth** and exerciseth **faith**, and bringeth forth **good works**, and **prayeth continually without ceasing**-unto such it is given to know the **mysteries of God**; yea, unto such it shall be given to **reveal things** which have never been revealed; yea, and it shall be given unto such to bring thousands of **souls to repentance**, even as it has been given unto us to bring these our brethren to repentance.*" (Alma 26:22)

In the D&C 42:61, the prophet Joseph Smith recited the Lord's words, *"If thou shalt **ask,** thou shalt **receive** revelation upon revelation, knowledge upon knowledge, that thou mayest **know the mysteries** and peaceable things that which **bringeth joy,** that which bringeth **life eternal.**"*

Alma 34:27 reads, *"Yea, and when you do not cry unto the Lord, let your hearts be full, drawn out in **prayer unto him continually** for your welfare, and also for the welfare of those who are around you."*

1 Thessalonians 5:16-23, *"**Rejoice** evermore. **Pray without ceasing.** In every thing give **thanks:** for this is the will of God in Christ Jesus concerning you. **Quench not** the Spirit. **Despise not** prophesyings. Prove **all** things; **hold fast** that which is good. **Abstain** from all appearance of evil. And the very God of peace **sanctify you wholly;** and I pray God your whole spirit and soul and body be preserved **blameless** unto the coming of our Lord Jesus Christ."*

Every time we partake of the sacrament, we covenant to *"always remember Him."* So by striving to keep a prayer in our hearts always, we more fully keep this sacred covenant. In return, the Lord will pour out the marvelous blessing He promises us, that we *"may always have his Spirit to be with us"* and the Holy Ghost will be our constant companion.

There is also great protection promised to those who pray always, in the following scriptures. Alma 13:28, *"But that ye would **humble** yourselves before the Lord, and call on his holy name, and watch and **pray continually,** that ye **may not be tempted** above that which ye can bear, and thus be **led by the Holy Spirit, becoming humble, meek, submissive, patient, full of love and all long-suffering"***

D&C 10:5, *"**Pray always,** that you may come **off conqueror;** yea, that you may conquer Satan, and that you may escape the hands of the servants of Satan that do uphold his work."*

We are also taught by the Lord to pray against Satan in these scriptures; Alma 34:22-23, *"Yea, cry unto him against the power of your enemies. Yea,* *cry unto him **against the devil**, who is an enemy to all righteousness."* The following scriptures are part of the account, when Moses commanded Satan to depart; *"…Nevertheless, **calling upon God,** he received **strength,** and he commanded, saying: Depart from me, Satan, for this one God only will I worship, which is the God of glory. And now Satan began to tremble, and the earth shook; and Moses **received strength,** and **called upon God,** saying: **In the name of the Only Begotten, depart hence, Satan**….And it came to pass that when Satan had departed from the presence of Moses, that Moses lifted up his eye unto heaven, being **filled with the Holy Ghost,** which beareth record of the Father and the Son;"* (Moses 1:20, 21, 24)

Elder Joseph F. Merrill in the April conference of 1941, p.50-51 said, *"Brethren and sisters, let us not be deceived. There are many agents of Satan abroad in the land and some of them may be **self-deceived**, **not knowing** that they are in the **power of the evil one.** However, the spirit of the devil among this people may be detected by all honest, sincere members who keep the commandments of the Lord. **The spirit of the Lord is comforting, joy-producing, love-inspiring, help-giving.** The spirit of the devil is manifested in fault-finding, envy, selfishness, hatred, deceit, dishonesty, and produces misery, sin and crime…In the spirit of helpfulness let me give you a key. When in doubt go on your knees in humility with an open mind and a pure heart with a real desire to do the Lord's will, and pray earnestly and sincerely for divine guidance. Persist in praying in this way until you get an answer that fills your bosom with joy and satisfaction. It will be God's answer. If obedient to this answer you will always act as the President indicates. You will then be safe."*

In 2 Nephi 32:8-9, *"…For if ye would hearken unto the Spirit which teacheth a man to pray ye would know that ye must pray; for the **evil spirit** teacheth not a man to pray, but **teacheth him that he must not pray.** But behold, I say unto you that **ye must pray always**, and not faint; that ye must not perform any thing unto the Lord save in the first place ye shall pray unto the Father in the name of Christ, that he will **consecrate** thy performance unto thee, that thy performance may be for the welfare of thy soul."*

President Brigham Young taught that, *"If the Devil says you cannot pray when you are angry,* **tell him it is none of his business**, *and* **pray** *until that species of* **insanity is dispelled** *and* **serenity is restored to the mind.***"* (JD 10:175)

President Joseph F. Smith said, *"Prayer does not consist of words altogether. True, faithful, earnest prayer consists more in the* **feeling that rises from the heart** *and from the inward desire of our spirits to supplicate the Lord in* **humility** *and in* **faith**, *that we may receive his blessings. It matters not how simple the words may be, if our* **desires are genuine** *and we come before the Lord with a* **broken heart** *and a* **contrite spirit** *to ask Him for that which we need…Do not learn to pray with your lips only. Do not learn a prayer by heart, and say it every morning and evening. That is something I dislike very much. It is true that a great many people fall into the* **rut of saying over a ceremonious prayer**. *They begin at a certain point, and they touch at all the points along the road until they get to the winding up scene; and when they have done, I do not know whether the prayer has ascended beyond the ceiling of the room or not."* (CR Oct. 1899, p. 69, 71-72) LDPDC 1:95-96

President George Albert Smith in the October conference of 1944, p. 95 stated, *"Reference has been made in this conference to the importance of seeking the Lord in prayer. And we should know that* **our prayers will not avail us much unless we repent of our sins**. *Faith, repentance, baptism by immersion for the remission of sins, laying on of the hands for the gift of the Holy Ghost, are the fundamental teachings of our Heavenly Father to us, and have been the groundwork of the Church since it was organized."*

President Heber J. Grant said, *"The prayerful and humble man will always realize and* **feel that he is dependent upon the Lord** *for every blessing that he enjoys, and in praying to God he will not only* **pray for the light** *and the* **inspiration** *of His Holy Spirit to guide him, but he will feel to* **thank Him** *for the blessings that he receives, realizing that life, that health, that strength, and that all the intelligence which he possesses come from God, who is the Author of his existence. If we do not keep this channel of communication open between us and our Heavenly Father, then are we robbed of the light and inspiration of His Spirit, and of that* **feeling of gratitude** *and* **thanksgiving that fills our**

*hearts and that **desire to praise God** for His goodness and mercy to us.*"
("Personal and Family Prayer" Dec 1942:779, TLDP 489)

Elder Marion G. Romney said, "*Frequently, prayers are requests for specific blessings. They may, however, and **should, include expressions of thanksgiving, praise, worship, and adoration.**"* (CR Apr. 1978 p. 73)

There are many wonderful verses of gratitude and praise to the Lord in the books of Psalms and Proverbs. These scriptures can inspire and teach us to praise and thank our Father in Heaven more fervently. For example Psalm 48:9-11 reads, "*We have thought of thy **loving -kindness, O God,** in the midst of thy temple. According to thy name, O God, so is thy praise unto the ends of the earth: thy right hand is **full of righteousness.** Let mount Zion **rejoice,** let the daughters of Judah be glad, because of thy judgments.*" and in Psalm 105:1-5, "***O Give thanks unto the Lord;** call upon his name: make known his deeds among the people. Sing unto him, **sing psalms** unto him: talk ye of all his wondrous works. **Glory** ye in his holy name: let the heart of them **rejoice that seek the Lord.** Seek the Lord, and his strength; **seek his face** evermore. Remember his marvelous works that he hath done; his wonders, and the judgments of his mouth.*"

President John Taylor said, "*Do not forget to call upon the Lord in your family circles, **dedicating yourselves** and all you have to God every day of your lives; and **seek to do right**, and cultivate the spirit of **union** and **love,** and the **peace** and blessing of the Living God will be with us, and He will **lead us** in the paths of life; and we shall be sustained and **upheld by all the holy angels** and the ancient patriarchs and men of God, and the veil will become thinner between us and our God, and we will **approach nearer to him**, and our souls will magnify the Lord of hosts.*" (JD 20:361)

The Prophet Joseph Smith in receiving the words of the Lord said, "***Pray always,** and I will **pour out my Spirit** upon you, and **great** shall be your blessing-yea, even more than if you should obtain treasures of earth and corruptibleness to the extent thereof. Behold, canst thou read this without **rejoicing** and lifting up thy heart for **gladness?** Or canst thou run about longer **as a blind guide?** Or canst thou be **humble** and **meek,** and conduct thyself **wisely** *before me? Yea, **come unto me thy Savior.** Amen."* (D&C 19:38-41)

Elder Neal A Maxwell wrote, *"Petitioning in prayer has taught me, again and again, that the **vault of heaven** with all its blessings is to be opened only by a combination lock. One tumbler falls when there is **faith**; a second when there is personal **righteousness**; the third and final tumbler falls only when what is sought is, in **God's judgment** -not ours-**right for us**. Sometimes we pound on the vault door for something we want very much and wonder why the door does not open. We would be very **spoiled children** if that **vault door opened any more easily** than it does. I can tell, looking back, that God truly loves me by inventorying the petitions He has refused to grant me. Our rejected petitions tell us much about ourselves but also much about our flawless Father."* (DGSM:34)

President Joseph F. Smith stated, *"We should live so **near to the Lord,** be so **humble** in our spirits so tractable and pliable, under the **influence of the Holy Spirit,** that we will be **able to know** the mind and will of the Father concerning us as individuals and as officers in the Church of Christ under all circumstances. And when we live so that we can hear and **understand the whisperings** of the still small voice of the Spirit of God, let us **do whatsoever the Spirit directs,** without fear of the consequences."* (CR Oct. 1903:86)

President Brigham Young stated, *"If we draw near to him, **he will draw near to us**; if we seek him early, we shall **find him**; if we **apply our minds faithfully** and diligently day by day, to know and understand the mind and will of God, it is as easy as, yes, I will say easier than it is to know the minds of each other, for to know and understand ourselves and our own being is to **know** and **understand God** and his being."* (JD13:312)

Elder John A Widtsoe said, *"If we want something for this Church and Kingdom, or if we want something for our individual lives, we must have a great, **earnest, overpowering desire** for that thing.* (such as being spiritually born of God) *We must reach out for it, with **full faith** in our Heavenly Father that the gift may be given us. Then it would seem as if the Lord himself can not resist our petition. If our desire is strong enough, if our whole will is tempered and attuned to that which we desire, if our lives make us **worthy of the desired*** *gift, the Lord, by his own words, is bound to give us that which we desire, in his own time and in his own manner."* (CR Apr. 1935:82) (parenthesis added)

In 2 Chronicles 7:14, *"If my people, which are called by my name, shall **humble** themselves, and **pray**, and **seek my face**, and **turn from their wicked ways;** then will I hear from heaven, and will **forgive their sin, and will heal their land.***"

The Lord, God Omnipotent, knows you and loves you with an overwhelming, personal love. He longs for you to come to Him, to open the door to your heart and let Him in, let Him heal you. Let Him become your closest and dearest friend! He loves so dearly, it is as if you were His only child. Love Him with all of your heart. Have no other gods before you, for He is jealous of all of the things that keep you from loving Him and spending time with Him. Patiently, He waits at the door to your heart. Let Him in, let Him in, let Him bind up your broken heart, and bless you with the marvelous gift of being spiritually born of God!

# CHAPTER 11

# *"Whoso Confesseth...Shall Have Mercy"*

*"He that covereth his sins shall not prosper: but whoso confesseth and forsaketh them shall have mercy"* Proverbs 28:13

President Joseph F. Smith said, *"...the moment a community begins to be* **wrapt up with themselves,** *become selfish, become* **engrossed in the temporalities** *of life, and put their* **faith in riches,** *that moment the power of God begins to withdraw from them, and* **if they repent not the Holy Spirit will depart from them entirely,** *and they will be left to themselves. That which was given them will be taken away, they will lose that which they had, for* **they will not be worthy of it.** *God is just as well as merciful, and we need not expect favors at the hand of the Almighty except as we merit them, at least in the honest desire of our hearts, and the* **desire and intent will not always avail unless our acts correspond.** *For we are engaged in a literal work, a reality; and we must practice as well as profess. We* **must be what God requires us to be,** *or else we are* **not his people** *not the Zion which he designed to gather together and to build up in the latter days upon the earth."* (JD, Apr 8, 1883, 24:176)

In section 19:20-21 of the Doctrine and Covenants, the Lord said, *"Wherefore, I command you again to repent, lest I humble you with my almighty power; and that you* **confess your sins, lest you suffer these punishments** *of which I have spoken, of which in the smallest, yea, even in the least degree you have tasted at the time I withdrew my Spirit. And I command you that you* **preach naught but repentance.***"*

1 John 1:8-9 it reads, *"If we say that we have no sin, we deceive ourselves, and the truth is not in us. If we **confess our sins**, he is faithful and just to forgive us our sins, and to **cleanse us from all unrighteousness.***" Confessing our sins to God is reiterated many times in the scriptures.

In the D&C 58:43 we read, *"By this ye may know if a man repenteth of his sins-behold, he will **confess them** and **forsake them.***" In D&C 64:7, 10 the Lord says, *" unto you, I, the **Lord, forgive sins** unto those who **confess their sins before me** and ask forgiveness, who have **not sinned unto death…***I, the Lord, will forgive whom I will forgive, but of you it is required to forgive all men."* And in Moisah 26:29 we read, *"…**if he confess his sins** before thee and me, and repenteth in the sincerity of his heart, him shall ye forgive, and I will forgive him also."*

In the D&C 29:43-44, 49 the Lord declares, *"And thus did I, the Lord God, appoint unto man the days of his probation-that by his natural death he might be raised in immortality unto eternal life, even as many as would believe; And they that believe not unto eternal damnation; for they **cannot be redeemed from their spiritual fall, because they repent not;** And, again, I say unto you, that whoso **having knowledge, have I not commanded to repent?***"

Elder James E. Talmage wrote, *"Revelation in the current age confirms the earlier scriptures in emphasizing the fact that **mortality is the probationary state**, and that the individual achievements or forfeitures **in this life** will be of eternal effect, notwithstanding the merciful provision made for advancement in the hereafter. The celestial kingdom of glory and eternal communion with God and Christ is provided for those who **obey the Gospel when they learn of it.***" ("The Vitality of Mormonism", p 258-59, LPDC Vol. 2, 465) *"And again, believe that ye must **repent of your sins** and **forsake them**, and **humble** yourselves before God; and ask in **sincerity of heart** that he would forgive you; and now, if you believe all these things see that ye do them."* (Mosiah 4:10)

In Alma 34:16-19, 27, *"And thus mercy can satisfy the demands of justice, and encircles them in the arms of safety, while he that **exercises no faith unto repentance** is exposed to the **whole law of the demands of justice**; therefore* only unto him that has **faith unto repentance** is brought about the great and eternal plan of redemption. Therefore may God grant unto you, my brethren, (of the church) that ye may begin to **exercise your faith unto repentance**, that ye begin to call upon his holy name, that he would have mercy upon you; Yea, **cry unto him for mercy;** for he is mighty to save. Yea, **humble yourselves,** and continue in prayer unto him…Yea, and when you do not cry unto the Lord, let your hearts be full, drawn out in **prayer unto him continually** for your welfare, and also for the welfare of those who are around you." (parenthesis added)

In Alma 42:29-30, we are told, "And now, my son, I desire that ye should let these things trouble you no more, and only **let your sins trouble you,** with that trouble which shall **bring you down unto repentance.** O my son, I desire that ye should deny the justice of God no more. **Do not endeavor to excuse yourself** in the **lest point because of your sins, by denying the justice of God;** but do you let the justice of God, and his mercy, and his long-suffering have full sway in your heart; and let it bring **you down to the dust in humility.**"

Omni 1:26, "And now, my beloved brethren, I would that ye should come unto Christ, who is the Holy one of Israel, and partake of his salvation, and the power of his redemption. Yea, **come unto him,** and **offer your whole souls** as an **offering unto him** and continue in **fasting** and **praying,** and **endure to the end;** and as the Lord liveth ye will **be saved.**"

Elder Marion G. Romney in the October conference of 1955 stated, "…there is rest in Christ for all whose **godly sorrow** brings them to **that repentance** which worketh salvation. Forgiveness is as wide as repentance. Every person will be **forgiven for all the transgression of which he truly repents.** If he repents of **all** his sins, he shall stand **spotless** before God because of the atonement of our Master and Savior, Jesus Christ, while he that exercises no faith unto repentance remains "…as though there had been **no redemption made** except it be the loosing of the bands of death." (Alma 11:41)

President Ezra Taft Benson said, "**Godly sorrow is a gift of the Spirit.** It is a deep realization that our actions have offended our Father and our God. It is the sharp and keen awareness that **our behavior caused the Savior,** He who *knew no sin, even the greatest of all, to endure **agony** and **suffering**. Our sins caused Him to bleed at every pore. This **very real mental** and **spiritual anguish** is what the scriptures refer to as having a 'broken heart and a contrite spirit'.* (3 Nephi 9:20; Moro. 6:2; D&C 20:37; 59:8; Psalms 34:18; 51:17; Isa. 57:15) *Such a spirit is the absolute **prerequisite for true repentance**"* (Ensign, Oct. 1989, p. 4)

In 2 Nephi 2:7 we are taught, *"Behold, he offereth himself a sacrifice for sin, to answer the ends of the law, unto all those who have a broken heart and a contrite spirit; and unto **none else can the ends of the law be answered.**"*

In Bruce R McConkie's book, "Doctrine and Covenants Commentary" p. 35 states, *"Repentance-That is the **message of the gospel to this generation.** Repentance is a complete change of mind, which brings about an equally **complete change of practice** as far as wrong doing is concerned. He who truly repents is sorry because of his sins, and **ceases sinning**. If he has wronged anyone, he **rights the wrong done**, as far as lies in his power to do so. He **confesses his sins** to God and to those whom he may have injured, and makes whatever restitution he can. That is true repentance."*

Elder James E. Talmage in his book the "ARTICLES OF FAITH" p. 99-100, he writes, *"**Nature of Repentance**—The term repentance is used in the scriptures with several different meanings, but, as representing the duty required of all who would obtain forgiveness for transgression it indicates a **godly sorrow for sin**, **producing a reformation of life**, and embodies (1) a **conviction** of guilt; (2) a **desire** to be relieved from the hurtful effects of sin; and (3) an earnest determination to **forsake** sin and to accomplish good. Repentance is a result of contrition of soul, which springs from a **deep sense of humility,** and this in turn is dependent upon the exercise of an **abiding faith in God**. Repentance therefore properly ranks as the second principle of the Gospel, closely associated with and immediately following faith. As soon as one has come to recognize the existence and authority of God, he feels a respect for divine laws, and a **conviction of his own unworthiness**. His wish to please the Father, whom he has so long ignored, will impel him to **forsake sin**; and this impulse will acquire added strength from the sinner's natural and commendable desire to **make reparation**, if possible, and so avert the dire results of his* *own waywardness. With the **zeal inspired by fresh conviction**, he will crave an opportunity of showing by **good works** the sincerity of his newly developed faith; and he will regard the **remission of his sins as the most desirable of blessings**. Then he will learn that this **gift of mercy is granted on certain specific conditions**. The first step toward the blessed state of forgiveness consists in the sinner **confessing** his sins; the second, in his **forgiving others** who have sinned against him; and the third in his showing his **acceptance of Christ's atoning sacrifice** by complying with the divine requirements…*

***The Sinner must be willing to forgive others,** if he hopes to obtain forgiveness. A man's repentance is but superficial if his heart be not softened to the degree of tolerance for the weaknesses of his fellows. In teaching His hearers how to pray, the Savior instructed them to supplicate the Father: "**Forgive us our debts, as we forgive our debtors.**" He gave them no assurance of forgiveness if in their hearts they forgave not one another: "For," said He, "**if ye forgive men their trespasses, your heavenly Father will also forgive you;** But if ye forgive not men their trespasses, neither will your Father forgive your trespasses." Forgiveness between man and man, to be acceptable before the Lord, must be unbounded. In answering Peter's question: "Lord, how oft shall my brother sin against me, and I forgive him—till seven times?" the Master replied: "I say not unto thee, until seven times: but, until seventy times seven;" clearly intending to teach that man **must ever be ready to forgive**. On another occasion He taught the disciples, saying: "If thy brother trespass against thee, rebuke him; and if he repent, forgive him. And if he trespass against thee seven times in a day, and seven times in a day turn again to thee, saying, I repent**, thou shalt forgive him**." The Lord has not promised to listen to petitions nor accept offerings from one who has bitterness in his heart toward others: "First be reconciled to thy brother, and then come and offer thy gift." In His revealed word to the saints in this day, the Lord has placed particular stress upon this necessary condition: "Wherefore, I say unto you, that ye ought to **forgive one another; for he that forgiveth not his brother his trespasses standeth condemned before the Lord; for there remaineth in him the greater sin**"; and to remove all doubt as to the proper subjects for human forgiveness, it is added: "I, the Lord, will forgive whom I will forgive, but of you it is **required to forgive all men**."*

On page 102 of the "ARTICLES OF FAITH" it reads, *"Repentance, to be worthy of its name, must comprise something more than a mere self-acknowledgment of error; it does not consist in lamentations and wordy confessions, but in the **heartfelt recognition of guilt,** which carries with it a **horror for sin** and a resolute determination to **make amends** for the past and to do better in the future. If such a conviction be genuine it is marked by that **godly sorrow** which, as Paul has said, "**worketh repentance to salvation,** not to be repented of; but the sorrow of the world worketh death."*

*Apostle Orson Pratt has wisely said, "It would be of no use for a sinner to confess his sins to God unless he were determined to **forsake them;** it would be of no benefit to him to feel sorry that he had done wrong unless he **intended to do wrong no more;** it would be folly for him to confess before God that he had injured his fellow man unless he were determined to do all in his power to make **restitution.** Repentance, then, is not only a **confession of sins,** with a **sorrowful, contrite heart,** but a **fixed, settled** purpose to **refrain from every evil way."***

***Repentance is Essential to Salvation**—This evidence of sincerity, this beginning of a better life, is required of every candidate for salvation. In the obtaining of divine mercy, repentance is as indispensable as faith; it **must be as extensive as sin.** Where can we find a sinless mortal? Sagely did the preacher of old declare: "**There is not a just man upon earth, that doeth good, and sinneth not.**" Who, therefore, has no need of forgiveness, or who is exempt from the requirements of repentance? God has promised **forgiveness unto those who truly repent;** it is unto such that the advantages of **individual salvation,** through the atonement of Christ, are extended. Isaiah thus admonishes to repentance, with assuring promises of forgiveness: "Seek ye the Lord while he may be found, call ye upon him while he is near: Let the wicked forsake his way, and the unrighteous man his thoughts: and let him return unto the Lord, and **he will have mercy** upon him; and to our God, for he will **abundantly pardon.**"*

The "ARTICLES OF FAITH" by Elder James E. Talmage on p. 103, exhorted us to repent when he said, *"**Repentance a Gift from God**—Repentance is* *a means of pardon and is therefore one of **God's great gifts to man.** It is **not to be had for the careless asking;** it may not be found upon the highway; nevertheless it is given with boundless liberality unto those who have brought forth **works that warrant its bestowal.** That is to say, all who prepare themselves for repentance will be led by the humbling and softening influence of the Holy Spirit to the actual possession of this **great gift.** When Peter was charged by his fellow worshipers with a breach of law in that he had associated with Gentiles, he told his hearers of the divine manifestations he had so recently received; they believed and declared: "Then hath God also to the Gentiles **granted repentance unto life."** Paul also, in writing to the Romans, teaches that repentance comes through the goodness of God."*

"ARTICLES OF FAITH" p. 105, Elder Talmage wrote, "**No soul is justified in postponing his efforts to repent** because of this assurance of longsuffering and mercy. We know not fully on what terms repentance will be obtainable in the hereafter; but to suppose that the **soul who has willfully rejected the opportunity of repentance in this life will find it easy to repent there** is **contrary to reason.** To **procrastinate** the day of repentance is to **deliberately place ourselves in the power of the adversary.** Thus Amulek taught and admonished the multitude of old: "For behold, this life is the time for men to prepare to meet God;…therefore, I beseech of you that ye **do not procrastinate** the day of your repentance until the end;…Ye cannot say, when ye are brought to that awful crisis, that I will repent, that I will return to my God. Nay, ye cannot say this; for that same spirit which doth possess your bodies at the time that ye go out of this life, that **same spirit** will have power to **possess your body in that eternal world.** For behold, **if ye have procrastinated** the day of your repentance even until death, behold, ye have become **subjected to the spirit of the devil,** and he doth seal you his.""

ARTICLES OF FAITH, p. 107 foot notes
Repentance
All mankind have need of repentance. If we confess our sins God is just to forgive—1 John 1:8, 9; see also Rom. 3:10; Eccl. 7:20. Return unto the Lord for he will abundantly pardon—Isa. 55:7. Who turneth away from his wickedness shall save his soul alive—Ezek. 18:27. Proclaimed by John the Baptist: Repent ye—Matt. 3:2, 8;Mark 1:4; Luke 3:3. Preached by Jesus Christ: Repent: for the kingdom of heaven is at hand—Matt. 4:17; see also Mark 1:15;

2:17. Christ came to call sinners to repentance—Luke 5:32. Joy in heaven over the sinner that repenteth—Luke 15:7, 10. Repentance and remission of sins preached in his name—Luke 24:47. Penalty following nonrepentance—Rev. 2:5, 16; compare 3:19.Wo unto the inhabitants of the whole earth except they shall repent—3 Nephi 9:2.How oft will I gather you if ye will repent—10:6.Whosoever repenteth and is baptized shall be saved—23:5. Preached by the Apostles: They preached that men should repent—Mark 6:12. Repent, and be baptized every one of you—Acts 2:38; see also 3:19; 8:22. God commandeth all men to repent—Acts 17:30. Rejoicing over those who sorrowed to repentance—2 Cor. 7:9, 10. The Gentiles were granted repentance— Acts 11:18. Blessing to him who brings a soul to repentance—Jas. 5:20; see also D&C 18:15, 16. The Lord desirous that all come to repentance—2 Peter 3:9.Way prepared for all men if they repent—1 Nephi 10:18. To be well with Gentiles if they repent; whoso repenteth not must perish—1 Nephi 14:5. Repentant Gentiles to become covenant people; nonrepentant Jews to be cast off—2 Nephi 30:2; 3 Nephi 16:13. All nations to dwell safely in the Holy One of Israel if they will repent—1 Nephi 22:28. Days of men mercifully prolonged for repentance—2 Nephi 2:21. Space granted that men might repent; a probationary state, a time to prepare to meet God— Alma 12:24; 34:32. People of God to persuade all men to repentance—2 Nephi 26:27. A curse upon the land, and destruction of the people if they would not repent—Jacob 3:3. Believe that ye must repent—Mosiah 4:10.Repentance preached by Alma at Mormon— Mosiah 18:7, 20. Words of the Spirit: Except ye repent ye can in no wise inherit the kingdom of heaven—Alma 5:51; see also 7:14.Do not procrastinate the day of your repentance—Alma 34:32-35. To the repentant and faithful it is given to know the mysteries of God—Alma 26:22 O that I were an angel, to cry repentance unto every people —Alma 29:1, 2. Lord has power to redeem men from their sins because of repentance—Helaman 5:11. O repent ye, why will ye die?—7:17.Would that I could persuade all ye ends of the earth to repent—Mormon 3:22. Repentance is unto them who are under  condemnation and the curse of a broken law—Moroni 8:24. Chastened that they might repent—D&C 1:27.Light to depart from him who repents not; Spirit of the Lord will not always strive with man—D&C 1:33; see also Moses 8:17.Every man must repent or suffer—D&C 19:4, 15.All men must repent, believe, worship God, and endure, or they cannot be saved—D&C 20:29. Call upon the nations to repent— D&C 43:20. May know if a man repenteth of his sins, he will confess and forsake them—D&C 58:43. Their sorrow shall be great unless they repent speedily—D&C 136:35. No one to be received into the Church unless he be capable of repentance— D&C 20:71. The thing of most worth to you will be to declare repentance—D&C 16:6; see also 18:15, 16. Adam and his immediate posterity were commanded to repent— Moses 5:8, 14, 15. Adam called upon his sons to repent—Moses 6:1. They called upon all men to repent—6:23; see verses 50, 57. Enoch called the people to repent— Moses 7:12. If men do not repent, I will send in the floods upon them—Moses 8:17; see verses 20, 24, 25.

President Spencer W. Kimball, in his book "Faith Precedes the Miracle" p.211 quotes Enos; *"and all the day long did I cry unto him;" Here is* **no casual prayer** *no worn phrases; no momentary appeal by silent lips. All the day long, with seconds turning into minutes, and minutes into hours and hours. But when the sun had set, relief had still not come, for repentance is not a single act nor forgiveness an unearned gift. So precious to him was communication with and approval of his Redeemer that his* **determined soul pressed on without ceasing.** *"yea, and when the night came I did still raise my voice high that it reached the heavens."* (Enos 4) *Could the Redeemer resist such determined imploring? How many have thus persisted? How many with or without serious transgressions, have ever prayed all day and into the night? Have many ever wept and prayed for ten hours? for five hours? for one? for thirty minutes? for ten? Our praying is usually measured in seconds and yet with a heavy debt to pay we still expect forgiveness of our sins.* **We offer pennies to pay the debt of thousands of dollars."**

In 2 Corinthians 6:10 we read, "*For* **godly sorrow worketh repentance** *to salvation not to be repented of: but the* **sorrow of the world worketh death.**" The "godly sorrow (which) worketh repentance" is very different from the "sorrow of the world" which is any of the following; being the victim, low self-esteem, depression, discouragement, hopelessness, helplessness, contention, confusion, anger, hate, fear, lying, resentment, selfishness, self-hate, lust, and pride, which "worketh death" because these things lead us away from Christ.

Godly sorrow, is coming to the Lord, with a grieving, "broken heart and a contrite spirit" and *"offer your whole soul as an offering unto Him."* In the depths of humility, confess **all** of your sins, and **plead** for forgiveness. In godly sorrow come to Him, and remember the incomprehensible, bitter pain, Jesus suffered to pay for **your** sins, and transgressions. He knows all of the thoughts, words and deeds that you need to repent of. And He **willingly suffered** to pay for them all.

Can you imagine, in vivid detail, seeing your Savior, your friend, your Lord Jesus Christ suffering in Gethsemane, with the tremendous weight of innumerable sins pressing down upon Him? Can you visualize Him, trembling and bleeding from every pour? Can you more fully realize that His blood was **shed for you,** for all of your sinful thoughts, words, and deeds? Can you image seeing your Redeemer, hanging on the cross in terrible agony, suffering intense pain, so that you might not suffer, if you will truly repent? Can you imagine coming to Him, in godly sorrow, and begging Him to forgive you for the pain you have caused Him?

*Jacob 1:8 ... "we would to God that we could persuade all men...to believe in Christ, and **view his death, and suffer his cross** and bear the shame of the world;..."*

*"But he was **wounded** for our **transgressions**, he was **bruised** for our **iniquities**: the chastisement of our peace was upon him; and with his **stripes** we are **healed**. All we like sheep have gone astray; we have turned every one to his own way; and the Lord hath laid on him the **iniquity** of us all. He was **oppressed**, and he was **afflicted**, yet he opened not his mouth: he is brought as a lamb to the **slaughter** ...He was taken from prison and from judgment: and who shall declare his generation? for he was cut off out of the land of the living: for the **transgression of my people was he stricken**."* (Isaiah 53:5-8)

*"...yea, remember that there is **no other way** nor means whereby man can be **saved**, only through the **atoning blood of Jesus Christ**, who shall come; yea, remember that he cometh to redeem the world.* (Helaman 5:9)

*"Therefore, whoso **repenteth** and **cometh unto me** as a little child, him will I receive, for of such is the kingdom of God. Behold, for such I have **laid down my life**, and have taken it up again; therefore **repent**, and come unto me ye ends of the earth, and **be saved**."* (3 Nephi 9:22)

Godly sorrow will lead us to truly "come unto Christ". It is an **essential part of** *"that repentance"* which leads us to salvation. *"They that sow in tears shall reap in joy."* (Psalm 126:5) Sow in tears of godly sorrow your confession to the Lord, and in time, you shall reap exceeding great joy, which comes to those who have had all of their guilt, and remorse swept away, having been spiritually born of God.

# CHAPTER 12

# "The Greatest of all the Gifts of God"

*"If thou wilt do good, yea, and hold out faithful to the end, thou shalt be saved in the kingdom of God, which is the greatest of all the gifts of God; for there is* **no gift greater than the gift of salvation.** *"* (D&C 6:13)

President Wilford Woodruff said, *"Now if you have the Holy Ghost with you and everyone ought to have-I can say unto you that there is* **no greater gift,** *there is no greater blessing, there is no greater testimony given to any man on earth. You may have the administration of angels; you may see many miracles; you may see many wonders in the earth; but I claim that the gift of the Holy Ghost is the* **greatest gift that can be bestowed upon man.** *"* (Deseret Weekly, April 6, 1889 p.451 TLDP: 275)

Elder Orson F. Whitney, in the Oct conference of 1929, p. 30 stated, *"God's greatest gift is eternal life, but that pertains to Eternity. The* **greatest blessing** *that our Heavenly Father can bestow upon us* **in time or while we are here,** *is the power to lay hold upon eternal life. The everlasting Gospel, through* **obedience** *to its* **every requirement,** *and the* **gift of the Holy Ghost, gives this power.** *It not only* **saves-it exalts** *men to where God and Christ dwell in the fulness of celestial glory."*

Elder John A. Widtsoe wrote, *"The more* **completely** *law is obeyed, the greater the consciousness of* **perfect joy.** *Throughout eternal life, increasing intelligence is attained, leading to greater adaptation to law, resulting in* **increasingly** *greater joy. Therefore it is **eternal life that is the greatest gift of God**, and that the plan of salvation is priceless.*" (A Rational Theology p. 34, TLDP: 320)

In the Doctrine & Covenants 14:5-8, the Lord tells us, "*Therefore, if you will **ask of me you shall receive**; if you will knock it shall be opened unto you. Seek to bring forth and establish my Zion. **Keep my commandments in all things.** And, if you keep my commandments and endure to the end you shall have **eternal life**, which gift is the **greatest of all the gifts of God**. And it shall come to pass, that if you shall ask the Father in my name, **in faith believing, you shall receive the Holy Ghost,** which giveth utterance, that you may stand as a witness of the things of which you shall both hear and see, and also that you may **declare repentance unto this generation.**"*

Elder Bruce R. McConkie stated, "*As starving men crave a crust of bread, as choking men thirst for water, so do the **righteous yearn for the Holy Ghost**. The Holy Ghost is a **Revelator**; he is a **Sanctifier**; he reveals truth, and he **cleanses** human souls. He is the Spirit of Truth, and his baptism is one of fire; he burns dross and **evil out of repentant souls** as though by fire. The gift of the Holy Ghost is the greatest of all the gifts of God, as pertaining to this life; and **those who enjoy that gift here and now, will inherit eternal life hereafter**, which is the greatest of all the gifts of God in eternity.*" (The Mortal Messiah, 2:122)

President David O. McKay said, "*Salvation is an individual operation. I am the only person that can possibly save myself. **When salvation is sent to me, I can reject or receive it.** In receiving it, I **yield implicit** and **submission** to its great Author throughout my life, and to those whom he shall appoint to instruct me; in rejecting it, I follow the dictates of my own will preference to the will of my Creator.*" (CR, Apr. 1957, p 7-8)

Elder Marion G. Romney wrote, "*In one sense, **repentance is the keystone** in that arch. Unless followed by repentance, professed faith in the Lord Jesus Christ is impotent; unless preceded by repentance, baptism is a futile mockery, effecting **no remission of sins**; and **without repenting, no one actually receives the companionship** of the Holy Spirit of God, notwithstanding the **laying on of hands** for the gift of the Holy Ghost.*" ("Look to God and Live" p 88-89)

The Prophet Joseph Smith said, "...*You might as well baptize a bag of sand as a man, if not done in view of the remission of sins and getting of the Holy Ghost. Baptism by water is but **half a baptism**, and is **good for nothing** without the other half-that is, the **baptism of the Holy Ghost**. The Savior says, "Except a man be born of water and of the Spirit, he cannot enter into the kingdom of God." Though we or an angel from heaven, preach any other gospel unto you than that which we have preached unto you, let him be accursed,*" (according to Galatians 1:8 (July 9, 1843.) DHC 5:498-500, TPJS p 314)

"***The baptism of water, without the baptism of fire and the Holy Ghost attending it, is of no use; they are necessarily and inseparably connected. An individual must be born of water and the Spirit in order to get into the kingdom of God.***" (TPJS p 360)

Elder Marion G. Romney also said, "*Each individual who observes one or more of these laws shall receive the blessings predicated thereon, and each Church member who will, with **all the energy of his soul, diligently strive to live them all,** shall receive the blessings predicated upon such striving. **Eternal life,** the **greatest gift of God,** is that blessing, and it will follow the living of the gospel as the night the day regardless of statistics of averages, or of what others think or say or do, for the Lord Almighty himself has said that "...every soul who **forsaketh his sins** and **cometh unto me,** and **calleth on my name,** and **obeyeth my voice,** and **keepeth my commandments, shall see my face and know that I am.***" (D&C 93:1) (CR, Oct, 1956 p. 15-16)

President Brigham Young said, "*Though our interest is one as a people, yet remember, **salvation is an individual work;** it is every person for themselves. I mean more by this than I have time to tell you in full, but I will give you a hint. There are those in this Church **who calculate to be saved** by the righteousness of others.* (perhaps Pres. Young is also referring to those who compare themselves, with the degree of righteousness of the other church members, and believe that they are just as righteous, so they calculate that they will saved) *They will miss their mark. They are those who will arrive just as the gate is shut, so in that case you **may be shut out;** then you will call upon some one, who, by their own faithfulness, through the mercy of Jesus Christ, have* *entered in through the celestial gate, to come and open it for you; but to do this is not their province. Such will be the fate of those persons **who vainly hope to be saved** upon the righteousness and through the influence of brother Somebody. I forewarn you therefore to cultivate righteousness and faithfulness in yourselves, which is the only passport into celestial happiness.* (D&C 45:56-57 JD, Dec. 18, 1853, 2:132)

President Joseph F. Smith stated, *"God has not and will not suffer the gift of the Holy Ghost to be bestowed upon any man or woman, except through **compliance with the laws of God**. Therefore, no man can obtain a remission of sins; no man can obtain the gift of the Holy Ghost; no man can obtain the revelations of God; no man can obtain the Priesthood, and the rights, powers and privileges thereof; no man can become an heir of God and a joint heir with Jesus Christ, **except** through **compliance with the requirements of heaven**"* (Gospel Doctrine, 5th ed. p. 49-50)

President Joseph Fielding Smith said, *"We should all be grateful for the wonderful principle of repentance; **we all need it**. But we must not lose sight of the fact that the **celestial kingdom is reserved for those who are sanctified** and none others. (Read Mormon 9:3-4) Let it be remembered also that those who sin **must repent in this life**; if they die in their sins, unrepentant, then no matter what blessings they have received, they are **not reinstated**."* (Alma 34:31-35; 3 Nephi 12:20, 27:17-19) *"When a man and a woman, in all sincerity, enter into a covenant of marriage for time and all eternity and **after** they have "**overcome by faith**," and are "**just and true**"* (Sec.76:54) *the Holy Ghost-who is the Spirit of promise-bears record of, or ratifies that sealing. In other words, he **seals the promises** appertaining to the marriage covenant upon them. Now the Lord has said: "But there is a possibility that man may fall from grace and depart from the living God; therefore let the church take heed and pray always, lest they fall into temptation; Yea, and even let those who are **sanctified take heed also**."* (Sec. 20:31-34) (LDPDC Vol 4, p 404)

President Gordon B. Hinckley said, *"There is **no greater blessing** that can come into our lives than the gift of the Holy Ghost-the **companionship of the Holy Spirit** to **guide** us, **protect** us, and **bless** us, to go, as it were, as a pillar before us and a flame to lead us in paths of **righteousness** and **truth**. That* guiding power of the third member of the Godhead can be ours *if we live worthy of it."* (Boston Mass. Regional Conference, Apr. 22, 1995)

The First Presidency (Brigham Young, Heber C. Kimball, Jedediah M. Grant) stated: *"Finally, brethren, give heed unto the whisperings of the Spirit of the Lord, your God. **Be ye filled with the Holy Ghost;** let your **peace flow** like unto a river, without let or hindrance; be **merciful** and **kind** to the stranger, and **forbearing** to each other; be faithful to **keep your covenants**, and abide the **trial of your faith.** Be **humble** before the Lord your God and **keep his commandments**, and the veil of the covering will be **filled with joy** and rejoicing..."* (MS, July 8, 1854, 16:429-30)

Elder George F. Richards said, *"We are not only to **receive the Holy Ghost, being born again,** the way the Lord has designed that it should be and has been in the days of the primitive Church, but we are to live and **labor** as to have the **constant companionship of the Holy Ghost,** for he will **not dwell in unholy tabernacles."*** (CR, Oct. 1944, p. 88)

In the "Lectures on Faith" by the Prophet Joseph Smith, he said, *"Where shall we find a prototype into whose likeness we may be assimilated, in order that we may be made **partakers of life and salvation?** or, in other words, where shall we find a saved being?"* What better starting point could there be than this—*find a saved being and then seek to be like him. "For if we can find a saved being, we may ascertain, without much difficulty, what all others must be, in order to be saved."* **They must be like that individual or they cannot be saved.** *"We think that it will not be a matter of dispute, that two beings who are unlike each other cannot both be saved; for whatever constitutes the salvation of one will constitute the salvation of every creature which will be saved; and if we find one saved being in all existence, we may see what all others must be, or else not be saved."* The reasoning is sound; the logic is perfect; and the foundation is laid to introduce a Saved Being. *"We ask, then, where is the prototype? or where is the saved being? We conclude, as to the answer of this question, there will be no dispute among those who believe the Bible, that it is Christ: all will agree in this, that he is the prototype or standard of salvation, or, in other words, that he is a saved being."* The **Lord Jesus set the pattern** in *all things. He is the great Exemplar. His command is that we should be as he is. If he gained salvation by treading the strait and narrow path, so must it be with us. "And if we should continue our interrogation, and ask how it is that he is saved? the answer would be—because he is a **just and holy being;** and if he were anything different from what he is he would not be saved; for his salvation depends on his **being precisely what he is** and nothing else; for if it were possible for him to change, in the least degree, so sure he would fail and lose all his dominion, power, authority and glory, which constitute salvation; for salvation consists in the glory, authority, majesty, power, and dominion which Jehovah possesses and in nothing else; and no being can possess it but himself **or one like him.**"* (Lectures on Faith 7:9.)

Returning to "A New Witness for the Articles of Faith" p. 149 by Elder Bruce R. McConkie, "***Salvation by Grace** (The Gospel Through the Ages, p. 10)*
*"Just what is meant by eternal life? We read in the Gospel of John that "this is life eternal to know Thee, the only true God, and Jesus Christ whom Thou hast sent." To know God is to have experienced His creative life to a large degree. Men must also **know the full meaning of love, mercy, forgiveness, justice, intelligence, chastity and goodness** in every respect by making those **attributes part of their lives.** In other words, they must through **obedience to every word** which comes from the mouth of their Heavenly Father **learn to become like God.** Regarding this subject, one of the eternal decrees of our Savior is as follows: Strait is the gate and narrow is the way that leadeth unto the exaltation and continuation of the lives....**If ye receive me** in the world, then **shall ye know me,** and shall receive your **exaltation;** that where I am ye shall be also. This is eternal lives—to know the only wise and true God, and Jesus Christ, whom he hath sent. I am he. Receive ye, therefore, my law.*

Elder Bruce R. McConkie stated in "The Mortal Messiah" 3 p. 81,
*"Accountable men, to gain salvation, must become as their little children. The refining powers of the gospel must operate in their lives. Sin and **evil must be burned out** of them as though by fire; they must receive the baptism of fire. They must be **converted—changed** from their carnal and fallen state to a state of righteousness, becoming again **pure and spotless** as they were in their infancy. Such is the **state of those who become heirs of salvation.** Then they will be*

*"greatest in the kingdom of heaven." That is to say, all who gain salvation, which is eternal life, shall be greatest in the kingdom of heaven,* **"for there is no gift greater than the gift of salvation."** *(D&C 6:13.) All shall inherit alike in that eternal kingdom; all shall be greatest, for they shall possess, inherit, and* **receive all that the Father hath.** *Thus, Jesus continues: Whosoever shall* **humble himself** *like one of these children, and* **receiveth me,** *ye shall receive in my name. And whosoever shall receive me, receiveth not me only, but him that sent me, even the Father.*

In "The Promised Messiah" which is also written by Elder McConkie on p.130 we read, *"Thus, to be saved, to gain exaltation, to inherit eternal life, to* **be one with God,** *to live as he lives, to think as he thinks, to act as he acts, to possess the same glory, the same power, the same might and dominion that he possesses.*

*Thus also, the Father is the great Prototype of all saved beings, and he and his Son, who also has become a saved being, are the ones into whose "likeness" Joseph Smith said we should be "assimilated." (Lectures on Faith, cited in Mormon Doctrine, 2nd ed., p. 258.) And thus, all those who overcome* **by faith,** *who become* **joint-heirs with Christ,** *who* **become one in him,** *as he is one in the Father, become themselves saved beings."*

In "Evidences and Reconciliations" pg. 32, John A. Widtsoe wrote, *"Brigham Young has furnished a definition in thrilling words: 'Salvation is the full existence of man, of the angels, and the Gods; it is eternal life, the life which was, which is, and that which is to come.' Life, then, is more than mere existence; it is "full existence."* **Life is active** *existence is static.* **Life is warm;** *existence, cold. Life uses its* **powers to secure progress; it moves upward.** *Existence is today where it was yesterday, or lower.* **Life is the increasing realization of man's highest ideals.** *The Lord Himself has made clear the distinction, for He said to Moses, "This is my work and my glory—to bring to pass the immortality and eternal life of man." (Pearl of Great Price, Moses 1:39) And Jesus, the Christ, made the same distinction when He said, "I am the resurrection, and the life." (John 11:25) Life in contradistinction to existence has always been the objective of Latter-day Saints. Life, implying a* **future of endless development,** *is the* **ultimate goal** *of the Church.*

*The Prophet Joseph Smith in his discourses gave added meaning to this defini-tion of salvation. "Salvation," he said, "means a man's being placed beyond the power of all his enemies" (Teachings of the Prophet Joseph Smith, p 301), and "**Salvation** is nothing more or less than to **triumph over all our enemies** and put them under our feet. And, where we have power to put all enemies under our feet in this world, and a **knowledge to triumph over all spirits** in the world to come, then we are saved, as in the case of Jesus, who was to reign until he had put all enemies under His feet, and the last enemy was death" (Teachings of the Prophet Joseph Smith, p. 297). There is no thought of iner-tia, mere existence, in such words. Instead, these statements imply action, a battle for **triumph over enemies** without and within....*

*"If salvation is eternal life as here defined, it may begin on earth, or may have begun in the pre-existent state of man. To the degree that a person uses his powers for **progress** on earth, and **lives fully under the law,** he is daily achiev-ing salvation and in a state of salvation. But, the summation of our efforts will be made on the great day of judgment, and will determine the degree of our salvation, our final place in the hereafter. This meaning of salvation is simple, easily understood. If the body is to be kept healthy, and fit for the work of life, certain definite laws must be obeyed. If the mind is to render full service, it must be properly fed and exercised. If the spirit is to **lift man into joy, spiritu-al tasks must be performed.** Only under such conditions of fully functioning powers can full life be lived. If salvation is to be gained, all the powers of life must be used, under the **laws of truth,** so far as in man's power lies. There must be a coordination of these powers for **steady progress.** As we seek salva-tion, an active eternal life, we must prepare ourselves for it by proper activity on earth."*

In the scriptures, oil often symbolizes the Spirit, as in the parable of the ten virgins as recorded in Matthew 25, beginning in verse 1. *"Then shall the kingdom of heaven be likened unto ten virgins, which took their lamps, and went forth to meet the bridegroom. And five of them were wise, and five were foolish. They that were foolish took their lamps, and took no oil with them:"* (they did not have the spirit as their constant companion) *"But the wise took oil in their vessels with their lamps."* (the wise will have the Spirit with them, because their inner vessels, their hearts are pure)…"*And the foolish said unto the wise, Give us of your oil…*" (each of us must grow in the steps to sanctification, because salvation is individual) "*Afterward came also the other virgins, saying, Lord, Lord, open to us. But he answered and said, Verily I say unto you, I know you not.*" Until we come to the Lord in godly sorrow and confess all of our sins to Him, and thus offer up an acceptable sacrifice of a broken, open heart to Him, we cannot know Him. Until we are born of God we cannot become His sons and His daughters and be known of Him.

In Matthew 7:21-23, and again in 3 Nephi 14:21-23, Our Savior said, "*Not every one that saith unto me, Lord, Lord, shall enter into the kingdom of heaven; but he that doeth the will of my Father which is in heaven. Many will say to me in that day, Lord, Lord, have we not prophesied in thy name? and in thy name have cast out devils? and in they name done many wonderful works? And then will I profess unto them, I never knew you: depart from me, ye that work iniquity.*"

Remember that no unclean thing can enter into the kingdom of heaven. So it will be with deep sorrow that the Lord will say, "*I never knew you, depart from me, ye that work iniquity.*" However, to those who have been spiritually born of God and have endured well to the end, God will say with exceeding great joy, "enter and receive thy glory!" May we be found worthy of the greatest of all the gifts of God, even life eternal with our Heavenly Parents and our Redeemer, Jesus Christ. Then it will be said of us; they "*shall inherit thrones, kingdoms, principalities, and powers, dominions, all heights and depths…and they shall pass by the angels, and the gods, which are set there, to their exaltation and glory in all things, as hath been sealed upon their heads, which glory shall be a fullness and continuation of the seeds forever and ever. Then shall they be gods, because they have no end; therefore shall they be from everlasting to everlasting, because they continue; then shall they be above all, because all things are subject unto them. Then shall they be gods, because they have all power, and the angels are subject unto them. Verily, verily, I say unto you, except ye abide my law ye cannot attain to this glory. For strait is the gate, and narrow the way that leadeth unto the exaltation and continuation of the lives, and few there be that find it, because ye receive me not in the world nei-*

*ther do ye know me. But if ye receive me in the world, then shall ye know me, and shall receive your exaltation; that where I am ye shall be also. This is eternal lives—to know the only wise and true God, and Jesus Christ, whom he hath sent. I am he. Receive ye, therefore, my law."* (D&C 132:19-24.)

In the holy, blessed name of Jesus Christ, Amen.

# *Appendix A*

## "The Reality and Power of His Atonement in My Life"

In June, 1974 I was baptized and confirmed a member of the Church of Jesus Christ of Latter-day Saints. It was a glorious experience and I remember it well. I never questioned the truthfulness of the gospel or of the Restoration. From the moment I heard the missionaries teach, I knew it was true. There was never even a flicker of doubt. It was like being reunited with an old and dear friend.

The spirit of repentance did not come upon me until the day I was baptized. Before that time I had received a testimony that the Gospel was true and that the Church of Jesus Christ had in fact been restored by the Prophet Joseph Smith. But the question of my sins had not been the object of my serious consideration until the day of my baptism. I was at the time, twenty-four years of age. For me, the process of repentance began with my baptismal interview prior to my baptism. The interviewer was kind and considerate although his questions pierced by soul. I wept as I confessed my sins and admitted my deep sorrow for my past life. My spirit was truly contrite as I entered into the waters of baptism. I wept openly throughout my baptism and confirmation as the spirit of the Lord testified to my heart of the tender mercies of a loving God. I had truly been born again to see the Kingdom of Heaven. I felt the burden of my sins lifted and I rejoiced with all my heart at my membership in Christ's true church.

Through it all, I did not know that, although I had received the spirit of repentance prior to my baptism, I had not received the gift of full repentance; that, while I had been born again to "see" the kingdom of heaven through the receipt of my testimony by the power of the Holy Ghost, yet I had not been born again to "enter" into the kingdom of God and I had not actually received the constant companionship of the Holy Ghost. While I had enjoyed a sanctifying experience that lifted the burden of my sins, yet I had not been sanctified unto a complete and unconditional remission of all my sins, including the effects of those sins. My knowledge of these heavenly truths did not come until later in July of 1981.

For seven years, from 1974 until 1981 I was actively and zealously engaged in gospel living. In December, 1975 my precious wife and I were married in the Arizona Temple. I was consumed with the desire to live the Gospel fully; to serve, teach, testify, study, and pray fervently. And I did so continually. I was actively involved in missionary work, temple work and home teaching. I strived to magnify all my church callings and took my membership in Christ's church very seriously, as I do to this day. I absorbed myself in gospel and scripture study, feeling that I couldn't read enough. I indeed hungered and thirsted after righteousness and truth and this hunger and passion has not subsided for even a moment, for even a heartbeat.

Through it all I enjoyed many spiritual experiences, sanctifying experiences. I have come now to describe such experiences as "contractions" leading to my spiritual birth. I felt the spirit of the Lord with me many times; I felt His love for me and felt a great love for Him and a desire to know Him. I was privileged to be an instrument in the Lord's hands several times in exercising the priesthood. Miracles were performed and lives were blessed. It was a wonderful seven years; a time of growth, development and preparation; a time of gestation. Yet through it all I sensed that something was missing. I could not describe what was missing in my life then, although now it is clear and understandable. Still, describing it to others is very difficult. It's like trying to explain the joy of parenthood to those who have never been parents.

In 1981 my life changed, for seven years the Lord had prepared my mind and my heart. My time was at hand. My Heavenly Father sent to me a son of God, a member of the church who was and is a true disciple of Christ, to draw me unto His Beloved Son. This blessed man carried within his soul the seed of Christ which he planted within my soul, the need and will to live spiritually. This is the endowment that ultimately induced the labor of the second birth.

The Spirit of the Lord bore witness to me that this man knew Christ. As we sat in my home one evening I felt the power of his testimony of the Savior as I had never felt it before. My soul was a flame with the desire to know the Lord as this man did, and I told him so.

The next morning as we were about to depart, my new friend boldly invited me to come to Christ. He urged me to pray more fervently until I received the baptism by fire; he called me to repent until I received a complete remission of my sins. His words were bold but kind and they sunk deeply into the core of my heart. The seed of Christ had been planted. Little did I know what all of this would mean.

This was a very difficult time in my life. At the time, I was serving as the Stake Mission President in my stake. I was immersed in my calling and was enjoying a good measure of success. But I was self-employed at the time and my consulting practice was very slow. In fact, at the time I had no clients and was financially without means to provide for my family. It was during this time that I was called to come home to Christ. Shortly after my friend departed I found myself in my office alone and without work. The Spirit called me one day as I sat behind my desk and prompted me to pray. I instructed my secretary that I did not want to be interrupted under any circumstances and then locked myself in my office and began to pour out my heart unto God. I prayed that day and for two succeeding days. I prayed long and hard and for many things. But the primary intent and focus of my prayers was to know the Lord and to understand and appreciate the personal implications of the atonement in my life.

On the third day, July 21, 1981, I found myself kneeling again by my chair in fervent prayer to know the Lord. Suddenly I saw myself praying and the presence of the Lord was beside me. As I watched, the Lord spoke to my mind and said, "Look" I looked and for the first time in my life I saw myself as I really was, through the eyes of Christ.

What I saw I can not fully describe in words. My whole soul was illuminated and I saw with complete clarity and understanding the deepest recesses of my subconscious mind. I saw within the hidden nooks and crannies of my soul the effects of all my sins as well as all my sins of commission and omission, which had been repressed into the hidden regions of my mind. I was completely transparent. Everything was now so painfully clear, my sinful motives, intentions and desires, all cleverly disguised and rationalized through years of self-talk. Even the good things I had done for the wrong reasons were flashed before my all-seeing eye. No act, word or deed escaped my view. I saw everything.

As I beheld myself thus, my mind was, to use Alma's words, "racked with torment" and "inexpressible horror." Several times I tried to shut out the vision but the Lord would not allow it. Each time I tried to turn away the Lord would say, "Look" and I continued to look into my soul. I wept and pleaded for the Lord to stop the vision. When I had finally seen everything the vision ended and there was darkness. I turned to find the Lord but He was no longer beside me.

The scene instantly changed and I found myself behind the brush on the outside of a garden clearing. Again a voice came to my mind and instructed me to look. My eyes turned to the garden clearing and there, in the midst, I saw my beloved Redeemer. Suddenly it became clear to me that I was witnessing His act of atonement. But what transpired I was not prepared to see.

 How can one explain with mortal words the agony of a God. Anything I say or write somehow diminishes the impact. Be that as it may, I saw the love and suffering of the Christ and I am a personal witness of it. I don't know how it is possible, but I was in Gethsemane on the day of His Agony and I saw in great and terrible detail with my eyes and heard in awful clarity with my ears that which is too sacred to describe to unprepared ears. His sobs and His cries pierced my soul and I felt the wrenching of my heart with each audible groan or quivering convulsion of His body. Then came the revelation that broke my heart: "Behold the love of God for you and His suffering for your sins."

It was too much to bear. As I became aware that He was suffering such agony for **me**, because of **my** sins, because of His love for **me**, for a "soul so rebellious and proud as mine", my heart broke and I thought I would die. Never had I sobbed and wept so violently and with such bitterness of soul. I never knew the body could sob as mine did. I never knew a heart could break as mine did. I never knew a broken heart would hurt as much as I hurt. I was in agony as never before. I thought my heart would stop and my head and chest would explode. I cried out and begged the Father to stop the suffering of my Friend and Elder Brother. "Stop it! Stop it! Please stop His suffering!" I wept, I sobbed and my body convulsed in anguish as I attempted to reach through the brush to hold Him, to somehow comfort Him. But His suffering did not stop and there was nothing I could do to help Him.

Finally, resolving myself to this hopeless state and wishing only to die for what I had done to Him, I cried out through my choking sobs, "Please forgive me! Please, dear God, forgive me for what I have done to my Savior. I am sorry, so very, very sorry for hurting Him so. It is enough," I continued, "please stop His suffering. I will never again do anything to hurt Him. Never! Never!"

I continued to sob and plead for forgiveness until I was totally exhausted and lay slumped on the floor weeping hot tears of anguish and pain. My strength was exhausted and I was prepared to die when the vision stopped and the voice of the Lord said unto me, "My son, thy sins are forgiven thee."

When I heard these words from my Savior I was filled with fire, which I later came to know was the endowment of charity. Never had I felt such love, such peace. I was overcome again unto great sobbing, but this time with joy. So intense was the outpouring of God's love through the fire of

His Spirit that I felt as though my very life would end and my flesh would be consumed. I came to know by the spirit of revelation that my life was acceptable to the Lord; that I had been completely and unconditionally cleansed of all my sins and the effects of my sins; that I had been made holy, without spot, clean every whit, by His precious blood. I had been truly born again to enter into the Kingdom of God; I was redeemed from the fall; sanctified by the endowment of His perfect love, even charity. Through this experience I came to understand the meaning of total conversion; of justification and of sanctification; and of full repentance.

I now know with a perfect knowledge that all men must be born again, or sanctified of the spirit, in order to receive their salvation and obtain their exaltation. I know now that only those who are truly born again can enjoy the blessings of the sanctified and can develop to the full stature of Christ. I now know that there is a difference between the righteousness of God and the righteousness of man; between full repentance and partial repentance; between a broken heart and a contrite spirit; between receiving forgiveness from one's sins and a complete and unconditional forgiveness from the effects of the fall of the natural man; between an awakening of conscience which cultivates a sense of duty to God and man and a mighty change of heart which bears the fruit of charity towards God and all men.

I now know that the only way to Christ is through the offering of a broken heart and that the only way to offer such a sacrifice acceptably is to experience, in a personal way, the power and reality of the Atonement in our life; to understand and appreciate sufficiently the personal implications of the sacrifice of Jesus Christ for our sins and fallen nature. Perhaps this may come in different ways to different people, but the substance and results of the experience will, of necessity, always be the same. The greatest manifestation of God's love for us is in the Savior's suffering for our personal sins. It is the power of His suffering for us that draws us to Him in a complete sense and changes our hearts totally. When our sacrifice of a broken heart has been accepted (i.e., justified) by the Lord, when we have fully repented of all our sins, then is our life acceptable (i.e., justified) unto the Lord. Sanctification, which is the effect or fruit of justification, totally cleanses and purifies the spirit and endows the person with a faith and hope in Christ, and with charity.

**The following is another unsigned personal testimony**

# "My 54 Week Journey"

I share this sacred account of my "born again" experience only that it may help another in his or her search to "come unto Christ." (Moroni 10)

My quest for a difference in my life began in 1981. I knew there was more spiritually than I was getting through my church meetings. I was dissatisfied with my Sundays, only learning from other people, and I began an in depth search of the scriptures. I read book after book, attended lectures, education weeks, and listened to devotionals. I had a hunger and thirst that could not be satisfied. I look back now and realize the yearnings I had were to lead me to the "mighty change."

I was so inexperienced in spiritual things I kept thinking my yearnings would be satisfied by books and other people's ideas, rather than going to my Heavenly Father in prayer, and using the scriptures more. The more I studied and learned with my head, deep in my heart I knew, that I knew nothing, especially about my Savior. There was more to the scriptures than stories and nice quotes, but they were sealed to me and they weren't the sealed portion! They were sealed because my eyes were blind and my ears were dull of hearing.

In 1986 President Benson gave a talk about the Church being under condemnation. I was part of that and it made me feel very uncomfortable. I didn't like being under condemnation from the Lord. This was the Lord's servant and mouthpiece and I took very literally what He said. I wanted that lifted off me, not just me but my family, friends, and everyone. My study intensified. Some days I studied more than others. We had several children during this time so my days were hectic, but I spent time daily in study and prayer.

In the fall of 1992, after unending locked doors in my spiritual searching, feeling like I almost had it, but because I lacked the pieces I had nothing, I heard a talk that held the key. I learned about the children of Israel and how they, like us, were under condemnation. I learned what they lacked was the willingness to let the Savior's gift work for them, they wanted to do it themselves (that explains the 600 plus commandments). The Savior's gift is-the atonement. How did it apply in my life? Where did I fit in all of this? I knew a lot about the gift in my head, but my heart did not understand.

I had some traumatic family events shortly after this that stripped me naked spiritually. There was nothing there. I felt like a stained glass window that had been pushed out of its frame and lay on the floor in hundreds of pieces. I had been studying for 12 years. I had much head learning, but my heart had barely been used.

The mourning, all but stopped my progress. I was numbed emotionally. I was in survival mode. I had no extended family support, my friends all left, and I was alone. What I knew in my head really didn't matter much. I learned how we are "nothing" without our Heavenly Father and His Son, our Redeemer. I knew what King Benjamin's message to his people about our "nothingness." (Mosiah 2)

In December of '93 I read a talk about prayer and overcoming false beliefs. I realized I didn't know how to pray. I had a lot of false beliefs cased by "traditions of the fathers and disobedience." (D&C 93:39)

For Christmas I received a copy of the book "Experiencing the Mighty Change" I read this book. So many bits and pieces I had studied were all put together under one cover (especially in part 2). This book literally saved me 20 more years of study. As I read this book, I realized this was what the Spirit, the study, and all the experiences were driving me towards. I didn't know what "born again" was. As I read the Book of Mormon, I discovered it was all through that holy book. No wonder President Benson was pushing us to read it. No wonder we were under condemnation. The scriptures began to open.

On December 2, I began my journey-the day I heard the talk on prayer. I began to pray about my false beliefs, the Savior, and my condemnation. Three weeks later, when I received the "Mighty Change" book, I began to pray about being born again, I also began to fast. I didn't know until I read this book that I didn't know how to fast either.

This journey was a very lonely one. At the time I knew of no one, who had had the born again experience except an author of one of the books I read. I called him several times (long distance so the calls were brief) to make sure I was on track, to see if the feelings I was experiencing were normal and other things. He was so kind to me. I could feel his goodness over the phone line. He strengthened me and I will be forever grateful to him for his help. I struggled so much because the path hadn't been cleared and very few people were willing to speak to me about the subject. Now I know it was because of ignorance. We all have our own experience so it is a new path for each one. But I also feel, to be strengthened by another is a great help during this most crucial and vulnerable time.

I decided I would fast every week. This was a challenge to me because I had blood sugar problems. I had to do it gradually but I now can fast a full 24 hours. Not only did I receive spiritual miracles, but physical miracles. What a blessing to have been healed from the blood sugar disorder, which I have been plagued with for years. What a wonderful blessing to participate in a true fast. It is a powerful testimony to me of the promises in Isaiah 58. Most important of all, the heavens were being opened to me.

I started getting up before my family every morning and I start having "mighty prayer." I used to think a mighty prayer was five minutes. What a privilege it is to talk to our Father at the beginning of every day and feel of His love for me and not count the minutes anymore.

As I began to do this, I was being taught what my false beliefs were, receiving revelation about original experiences which set them in place and tutored from on high and healed. Talk about counseling! I was made aware of my sins which were caused from these false beliefs (these come from disobedience or traditions of my fathers.) In Dec. 93, I was made aware of all my sins…all of them. I knew of the hurt I had caused others and the impediments upon my own growth. I saw myself as Christ can see us, all the cover-ups, the sneakiness, the honors of men syndrome, my condemnation of others, all my self-righteousness and everything that was my carnal man.

It was necessary for me to get some unlayering done. These were layers that were blocking the Spirit from being in full fellowship with me. It took a while for me to get through this process. I know now it was because I was mourning the deaths of three close loved ones and my heart had to go through the process slowly. I would feel the Spirit, the cleansing and all that comes with this for 1-2 hours a day, 3-4 days a week. My husband, on the other had, went through it in a few days with no let up.

I felt mourning for my errors and sins. This part of the experience was not fun. I was mourning because of the distance they had put between me and my God. The mourning was physical, mental, emotional, and spiritual. It was literal gut wrenching mourning and sorrow.

One day, as I was studying about the Savior, I saw Him in Gethsemane. This was my Lord struggling over the sins of the world, struggling over my sins. I saw Him, see me. I saw Him see my life. He saw all my filth and unworthiness and said, "Yes!!! I will do it!!! I love her!!!" He bought me with His blood. He did this for each person. As I watched Him I thought my heart would break. I felt as though my chest would explode. I sobbed as I felt His love and compassion for me. I felt His holiness, His goodness, His strength, His truth, His mercy. These words seem hollow to use, to describe Him. I couldn't bear to watch Him any more. "Dear God" I cried, "Please, I cannot see this anymore." I saw Him in agony a while longer, then the vision closed. I lay on the floor exhausted from what I had just witnessed.

My new life began with a wash of peace that filled and warmed my entire being. It was a feeling of burning throughout my whole body-but a sweet burning. The voice of the Lord came to me and said, "Your sins are forgiven." I didn't want to move. I could feel the warmth, the love, the joy, the total peace. I had the same experience the next morning and again on Sunday during the sacrament. December 16, exactly 54 weeks from the beginning of the journey. I turned it all over to the Lord. All of it, I gave to Him and He made me His! I knew my life was acceptable to Him. I was a new creature. I was gratefully His!

All the rest of my false beliefs He took. He took my sins. He took the condemnation I felt for myself and thus for others. He took all judgement from my heart, all the have to be's and need to be's and ought to be's. I remember these things and the accompanying state of being only when He brings it to my recollection. The guilt and torment, the heaviness and burden has been washed away.

I live for today. This moment of time and all is perfect in Him. I know the instant I do something offensive and take care of it or I do not do it, or say it. The Spirit does a wonderful job tutoring. I have been blessed with discernment, to see into the hearts of people I interact with and know their motives, whether righteous or evil. The scriptures are being opened to me.

I am at the beginning of my walk with God. (2 Nephi 9:41) I sing praises to Him. Without Him I am nothing, with Him I can do all He want me to do. He is God. He is truth. He is no respecter of persons. He is merciful. This is a gift for all, to be bestowed on all. In order to know the attributes of God and have them burned into your heart, you must receive this gift. In "The Lectures on Faith" Joseph Smith teaches about the attributes of God perfectly. This born again process teaches you these things about Him. The world is a different place. I see it through new eyes and with the gift of the new heart. Everything is perfect. We all experience what we need to bring us to Christ if we allow it to happen. God is merciful!!! He pardoned me!!! A sinner, and truly I, as the weakest of all His disciples, He makes me strong.

I pray that the love, light, joy of the Savior may be with you. If you haven't had this experience, it is worth the journey. For me I had to go to Hell and back and it is worth it!!!

I pray, whoever may read this account may feel His Spirit upon you even as the warmth of the sunshine. I know God is our Father. I know by my experience of this, and also of our Savior Jesus Christ. He loves us!!! He died for us!!! He lives for us!!!

I say this in the holy name of Jesus Christ. Amen

## This is another unsigned spiritual rebirth experience

# "Come Unto Him all Ye that…are Heavy Laden, and He Shall Give You Rest"

After being married to a very negative man for nineteen years, I began experiencing very serious heart problems. The overwhelming stress of having to deal with an anger-aholic husband, and family of teenagers was causing me to have chest pains, on almost a daily basis. I was at the end of my rope. I needed to know that the Lord would release me from this unbearable marriage. The only time I felt cherished, was the first month we were married, and I had planned an eventual divorce, for many years. Now, I needed the physical, emotional, and spiritual strength to escape this very hostile man, who was destroying my health and my children's happiness.

I came across a book that taught about the mighty change of heart, and I decided to fast every Sunday, beginning in July '94, I also began studying the scriptures more intently and I attended the temple 2-3 times each week. I learned to pray more continually, and my personal prayers were with all the sincerity of my heart. The more intently I prayed, the more I felt guided towards repentance even though I saw myself as a victim. The Spirit taught me that I was partly responsible for this awful relationship, and that I needed to do the Lord's will instead of my will. I needed to trust in the Lord's plan for me and my family.

Each time I attended the temple, my experiences drew me closer to the Lord. It was early in November 1994 when the following experiences happened. Each time I went to the temple I spent a long time in the dressing booth, pouring my heart out to Lord (In a manner similar to my recent prayers at home). I vividly imagined myself in the Garden of Gethsemane.

I visualized my Savior, trembling and bleeding from every pore. Then I plead with Father to forgive me, and I told Him how very sorry I was to cause this terrible pain to be poured down upon my Redeemer.

One by one, I was reminded of sins that I hadn't completely repented of. One by one, I saw drops of His precious blood fall to the ground for me. I prayed for forgiveness of each sin, (and outside of the Temple, I did many things to make amends.) After praying in my dressing booth, I would go into the initiatory area. Time and time again, as those beautiful words were said, my eyes would stream with tears of gratitude. The Spirit witnessed their fulfillment to me, and I was filled with exquisite joy, each time I heard these precious promises. At times the joy was so intense, I remember thinking "if the joy becomes any more intense, it might be painful." I usually stayed two hours, doing initiatory and during this time, I felt the sweet joy, and love of being filled with the Spirit!!! There were several temple working sisters, who became close spirit to spirit friends, even though I seldom said anything to them. I would leave the temple with an overwhelming desire to hug everyone I saw, and ask them if they had any idea how much the Lord loves them. The words from a hymn came into my mind, "cast our burdens upon the Lord and he shall sustain thee." I was so filled with joy that I wanted to sing praises to the Lord continually!!!

Each time I returned to the temple for the next two months. The experiences were so wonderful that I didn't want to leave. Each time, as sweet sisters anointed me I felt the Spirit of the Lord fill my entire being with intense love, and indescribable joy. Truly, He anointed my head with oil, my cup runneth over. I prayed to the Lord with every fiber of faith in my soul. Thanking Him for the many prayers He had miraculously answered. Thanking Him for healing my heart, (even before I noticed any change in my heart condition, I thanked Him). I also fervently thanked the Lord for His atoning sacrifice, and for the pain he suffered for me. I promised to consecrate my life to His work, and to do His will.

Before these experiences, I couldn't cope with my life the way it was, so I finally gave my life to the Lord. I told Him that I trusted Him, I knew He could make much more out of my life than I could. In my mind, I clearly heard the God's voice as he said the words, "Thy sins are forgiven thee" I felt completely forgiven of my sins and tears immediately filled my eyes, as the words were spoken. I felt the Saviors love fill my entire being. I visualized myself at His feet, thanking Him, and kissing His feet with my grateful tears. At times, it felt like His arms were around me, the intensity of the feeling of His perfect love is far greater than I have ever felt from anyone on earth. Even writing of it overwhelms me to tears. For His love is far greater than can be expressed in words. I know that my Redeemer lives, what rapture this sweet sentence gives!!! I know that He loves each of His children, individually unconditionally, and exquisitely!!!

I was also taught by the Spirit, how to let go of emotional pain, when difficult situations came up. I would go to a private place and visualized a thorny bush, which represented the many painful experiences of my past. The deep roots were the subconscious pain that I had forgotten. As I prayed, I imagined seeing the Lord, and I explained to Him that "I have tried to bury this bush with denial, I've tried to kill it with anger, I have tried to pull it out by myself. But I can't do it, by myself. Please help me please tear out the pain of my past." Then I imagined seeing His nail scared hands easily pull out my painful bush, of negative feelings and hold it out to me, because it was mine. I then begged Him to throw it away, so with one stroke of His mighty arm, He threw it far out into space. I watched as this bush of my pain and fear gradually disappeared. The Spirit then told me to "let it go, and let Christ atonement heal you." It was gone, all of the terrible feelings were gone!!!

I breathed in a feeling of peace and relief. Then I imagined I was knelling at Jesus' nail scared feet. I could almost feel His hands placed on my head, and the Spirit whispered to my heart, His words of intense, personal love! Then He blessed me so that all of the empty places where the pain use to be, to now be filled with His love and His light! I visualized myself filled with light! Then I imagined what it might feel like to be lifted up and held in His arms. To be encircled in the arms of His everlasting love. It was real! I was filled with such exquisite love, that tears of gratitude and joy streamed down my face.

The Spirit also taught me that anytime I was being mistreated, or had negative thoughts and feelings of the past come back into my mind, I could go to a quiet room and visualize this experience. I realized that within a few minutes, of this type of prayer, I could be relieved of anger, fear, and emotional pain, and be filled with peace, love, hope and the joy of the Spirit.

By the middle of November 1994, my chest pains disappeared and have never returned. My dear Savior healed not only my heart, but also my soul. For He truly healed me physically, mentally, emotionally, and spiritually!!! The painful thoughts of the past no longer hurt me. Finally, I realized that all of these awful experiences had a purpose, which was to bring me to Christ, in humility, and in desperate need, so that I could offer up an acceptable sacrifice to the Lord of a broken, penitent heart and a contrite spirit.

My greatest desire is to see my Lord, Jesus Christ, while I'm still on this earth, and to receive my calling and election made sure. I also pray that my children will always love truth, and that they will hunger and thirst after righteousness. That they may learn to open their hearts to the Lord in fervent prayer, and truly repent. I pray that they will study the scriptures daily, and be obedience to all that the promptings of the Holy Ghost. So that they may experience this blessed event of the baptism of fire, which purifies and burns out all desire to do evil, which sweeps away all guilt and blesses one with the desire to do good continually, to love God, and to serve Him with pure intentions and pure motives. Which also enlightens ones understanding, so that the scriptures come alive, with clarity that was never before possible. Which fills ones soul with a much greater appreciation for all that the Lord has given us, especially His words and deeds, which we are so blessed to have in the scriptures and through His prophets.

After my born again experience, I was surprised at how much I appreciated all of Gods beautiful creations, even the smallest insect or weed. One morning, as I was eating fresh strawberries, I suddenly realized that I had never really looked at a strawberries intricate design. I felt a great joy as I thanked the Lord for this delicious fruit .My senses and my emotions have become greatly enhanced.

I have also been blessed to see Heavenly Fathers children more clearly, and feel more love, and compassion for them. My intuition about people has increased. Sometimes the Spirit tells me what someone is thinking or feeling. I have also been blessed with the great gift of love, and frequently I feel an intense love for God's children. I have discovered that each time I pray for the Spirit to be with me, immediately I feel the sweet comfort of the Holy Spirit. I am so grateful for this marvelous gift, for the inspiration and guidance I receive whenever I pray sincerely for it.

I still make plenty of mistakes, and I try to repent quickly. I strive to have a prayer of gratitude in my thoughts continually. I can never thank my Savior enough for paying for my sins, for his grace, his gift of forgiveness, for sweeping away all my guilt and pain, and filling me with inexpressible joy, peace & love, for increasing my faith, hope and charity, and many other Christ-like qualities. All of these great blessings I am so undeserving, and yet I am so grateful.

The Lord has been so generous to me, and has blessed me with several choice friends, who have become the family I never had. I am so grateful for them, and their love. I finally feel understood, and appreciated.

After reading about my experiences, you may find it hard to believe that it wasn't until a few months after these marvelous things happened that I came to know that I had received the baptism of fire and the fullness of the Gift of the Holy Ghost. I didn't believe that this would happen until after I was released from this painful marriage, and my teenagers had grown up. How could I become worthy enough, while I was living with this very difficult husband, and was having to deal with him every day?

It was at a wedding breakfast, in the spring of 1995 where I met an author of a choice book that teaches the meaning of sanctification. As soon as I saw him, I felt the Spirit draw me towards him like a strong magnet. His gentle, humble countenance, reassured me that I could share, what the Spirit had constrained me from sharing with anyone until then. After listening intensely for several minutes, He looked into my eyes and told me that I had received the born again experience. The Spirit witnessed to me that it was true! I am certain that he was inspired to say this. (I believe that others in a similar circumstance would be wise to encourage the questioning person to get the answer from the Lord, to know if they have been truly born again, because they need to receive this answer from Him.

I had been like the Lamanites in 3 Nephi 9:20 "And ye shall offer for a sacrifice unto me a broken heart and a contrite spirit. And whoso cometh unto me with a broken heart and a contrite spirit, him will I baptize with fire and the Holy Ghost, even as the Lamanites, because of their faith in me at the time of their conversion, were baptized with fire and with the Holy Ghost, and **they knew it not**." I know that I had been blessed with a series of wonderful spiritual experiences but I didn't know that it was the baptisim of fire. I was expecting that when I someday received the great blessing of spiritual rebirth, that it would be similar to the ones I had read, and I didn't realize that it is unique for each person and yet there are some things that are always similar. Perhaps it is because the Lord knows our own unique language, personality and circumstances is why he communicates to us according to our understanding. Just as the accounts of those who die and come back, have unique experiences, and yet there are some things that are very similar.

Even though my husband and children know nothing of my experiences, they have noticed a vast difference in me. I act differently, and my intentions are focused on doing the Lord's will continually.

 Our bishop who was also our marriage councilor, looked stunned, when he saw me in church happily hugging almost everyone in the ward in Dec 1994.  Later he asked me what had happened, and I told him that the Lord has healed my heart, and swept away all of the regrets and pain of my past.

Three years later, I read the book "Following the Light of Christ into His Presence." It was so exciting to read that this author had been taught the same deeper understandings of the scriptures that the Spirit had been teaching me over the preceding 3 years. On countless occasions, the Spirit of the Lord has witnessed to me, that what I received was indeed the Born Again experience.

Everyday I still ask the Lord, "what would ye have me repent of," and the Spirit shows me, one by one my weaknesses. Then I confess them and strive to forsake them. The great love and joy I feel daily as I pray is indescribable.

In closing, I wish to express my gratitude to my Heavenly Father, for the abundant blessings he has given me, and my family. I am thankful to him for softening my husband's heart, and for guiding us to councilors, who have helped him. For assisting my children in recovering from growing up in a dysfunctional family, and for helping them grow in their testimonies. I can never express enough gratitude to the Lord for the countless prayers he has answered. And I am even grateful for the times he has answered me with a "No" because he knew what was best for me, and my family.

I Love my Savior, with all my heart, and pray that I may learn to love Him and all of God's children more perfectly. I can never thank my Redeemer, enough for rescuing my soul, for suffering unbearable anguish for me, a sinner. O it is wonderful! I pray that I may retain a remission of my sins, and always live my life, in a pleasing manner before the Lord. That I may continue to strive to have a prayer in my heart, and always remember Him, that I may always have His Spirit to be with me.

I say this in the holy name of Jesus Christ, Amen.

The next unsigned account is by a woman who experienced the baptism of fire and the Holy Ghost when she was confirmed a member of the Church.

# "My Experiment Upon the Word"

I was baptized on schedule, along with my husband and daughter. I received the gift of the Holy Ghost. There were three immediate changes which I noticed. First, the morning after my baptism, it was made clear to me that my ability to bear children had been restored, after a ten-year drought. Second, there was another unexpected change in my life! My "senses" expanded! It was as though someone had given me a pair of spiritual eye-glasses and a hearing aid! My vision was magnified, and my hearing amplified! I could see and understand virtually everything more clearly. Scriptures that had been unclear to me suddenly became clear and understandable. I could hear more depth and meaning into things people told me about themselves. As I listened, my compassion and love for others increased. I was newly amazed-all over again!

Third, after receiving the gift of the Holy Ghost, I received another new physical manifestation. I was standing in the hall telling a brother, part of my story of conversion. As I spoke, a strong tingling feeling started spreading through my body, from head to toe. It felt like mild electricity, only pleasant-from the top of my head, down through my spine, out my arms, and down to my toes. So unexpected was it, that it startled me. I had never felt such a thing before. I wasn't sure what it was. But it was amazing. Though it startled me, I said nothing about it to the person with whom I spoke. We talked on, and as we did, the brother then said something to me that I could tell had elements of "pure truth." Again, I felt the strong tingling sensation, and again was startled by it. When I arrived home, I decided to pray about it. Alone in my bedroom, I kneeled down and asked Heavenly

Father about it. Heavenly Father, since I've been baptized, I've noticed that when someone says something to me, or I to them that seems to be a "pure truth" of some kind, these tingles go through my body. Is that the Holy Ghost I'm feeling?"

The instant I asked the question, the answer came. In waves! Wave, after wave, after wave of tingles rushed over me and through me, like waves of water at the beach! My whole body was washed over and immersed in these tingling, spiritual "waves of witness!" Heavenly Father was answering my question with "Yes! Yes! Yes! This, my daughter, is the witness of the Holy Ghost to you! Whenever you feel this, you will know it is the Holy Ghost witnessing that what has been spoken is true." Just by being baptized and receiving the gift of the Holy Ghost, my body had been healed, my senses and abilities expanded, and a personal, divine witness that what is being spoken it true. I was being blessed and added upon in ways I had not expected, and in ways I hadn't even requested! What wonderful, unexpected gifts from a loving Father who delights to bless his children; from a loving Savior who had paid a high price for me, and a loving Holy Ghost, so eager to bear witness of the Father and the Son!

As Latter-day Saints we are the light of the world, as we reflect the Savior's light through us. Because we have the light of the gospel, we have a duty to all whose lives we touch. We have a duty to "stand for truth and righteousness" wherever we may be. As you will learn for yourself, the cost of standing for truth and righteousness may sometimes be high-but a personal relationship with Christ, and the joy of knowing Him and being worthy to associate with Him, is worth any sacrifice. And anything we "lose" in the process is replaced many times over by something of far greater value, eternal worth, and joy. When faced with a choice, whom will I love? Always choose "the good part" (2 Nephi 2:30)

To the end that we can strengthen one another, that we can encourage one another to choose life, to experiment upon the word, to hold fast to the iron rod, to bring joyful blessings upon your heads and upon the heads of your future children whose lives will be affected by your choices today, I share my testimony, with eternal love and gratitude in my heart to the Savior, who has provided a way for us to return Home.

I say these things in the name of Jesus Christ, Amen

**Another unsigned testimony**

# "It Was Written With His Blood"

In that place between wakefulness and dreams, I found myself in a room. There were no distinguishing features in this room save the one wall covered with small index card files. They were like the ones in libraries that list titles by author or subject in alphabetical order. But these files, which stretched from floor to ceiling and were seemingly endless in either direction, had very different headings. As I drew near the wall of files, the first to catch my attention was the one that read "Girls I Have Liked." I opened it and began flipping through the cards. I quickly shut it, shocked to realize that I recognized the names written on each one.

And then without being told, I knew exactly where I was. This lifeless form with its small files was a crude catalog system for my life. Here were written the actions of every moment, big and small, in a detail my memory couldn't match.

A sense of wonder and curiosity, coupled with humor, stirred within me as I began randomly opening files and exploring their content. Some brought joy and sweet memories, others a sense of shame and a shudder to see if anyone was watching. A file named "Friends" was the next to one marked "Friends I have Betrayed!"

The titles ranged from the mundane to the outright weird. "Books I Have Read." "Lies I Have Told." "Comfort I Have Given." "Jokes I Have Laughed At." Some were almost hilarious in their exactness. "Things I've Yelled at My Brothers." Others I couldn't laugh at: "Things I Have Done in My Anger." "Things I Have Muttered Under my Breath to My Parents" I never ceased to be surprised by the contents. Often there were many more cards than I expected. Sometimes fewer than I had hoped.

I was overwhelmed by the sheer volume of the life I had lived. Could it be possible that I had the time in my 40 years to write this truth? Each was written in my own handwriting. Each signed with my own signature.

When I pulled out the file marked "Songs I Have Listened To." I realized the file grew to contain their contents. The cards were packed tightly and yet after two or three years, I hadn't found the end of the file. I shut it, shamed, not so much by the quality of the music, but more by the vast amount of time I knew that file represented.

When I came to a file marked "Lustful Thoughts." I felt a chill run through my body. I pulled the card file out only an inch, not willing to test its size, and drew out a card. I shuddered at its detailed content. I felt sick to think that such a moment had been recorded.

An almost animal rage broke on me. One thought dominated my mind: "No one must ever see these cards! No one must ever see this room! I have to destroy them!" In an insane frenzy I yanked the file out. Its size didn't matter now. I had to empty it and burn the cards. But as I took it at one end and began pounding it on the floor, I could not dislodge a single card. I became desperate and pulled out a card, only to find it as strong as steel when I tried to tear it.

Defeated and utterly helpless, I returned the file to its slot. Leaning my fore-head against the wall, I let out a long, self-pitying sigh. And then I saw it. The title-"People I Have Shared Jesus' Teachings With." The handle was brighter than those around it, newer, only inches long, it fell into my hands. I could count the cards it contained on one hand.

And then the tears came. I began to weep. Sobs so deep that the hurt start-ed in my stomach and shot through me, I fell on my knees and cried. I cried out of shame, from the overwhelming shame of it all. The rows of files shelves swirled in my tear-filled eyes. No one must ever, ever know of this room. I must lock it up and hide the key.

But then, as I pushed away the tears, I saw Him. No, please not Him. Not here. Oh, anyone but Jesus. I watched helplessly as he began to open the files and read the cards. I couldn't bear to watch the look on His face, I saw a sorrow deeper than my own. He seemed to intuitively go to the worst boxes. Why did He have to read every one?

Finally, He turned and looked at me from across the room. He looked at me with pity in His eyes. But this was a pity that didn't anger me. I dropped my head, covered my face and began to cry again. He walked over and put His arm around me. He could have said so many things. But He didn't say a word. He just cried with me.

Then He got up and walked back to the wall of files. Starting at one end of the room He took out a file and one by one, began to sign His name over mine on each card. "No!" I shouted, rushing at Him. All I could find to say was, "No, no" as I pulled the card from Him. His name shouldn't be on these cards. But there it was, written in red so rich, so dark, so alive. The name of Jesus covered mine.

*It was written with His blood.*
He gently took the card back. He smiled a sad smile and began to sign the cards. I don't think I'll ever understand how He did it so quickly, but the next instant it seemed I heard Him close the last file and said, "It is finished."

 I stood up, and He let me out of the room. There was no lock on its door. There were still cards to be written.

# *Appendix B*

## "Sanctified take Heed Also"

President Joseph Fielding Smith stated; "Sanctification is also true. Through the praise of the Father, we may be sanctified from all a sin through acceptance of the gospel and compliance with all the ordinances. We are told that those "who overcome by faith, and are sealed by the Holy Spirit of promise, which the Father sheds forth upon all those who are just and true" will be entitled to become sons of God. (See D&C 76:53-54) and Moses 7:57-60) The Lord has said: "But there is a possibility that even those who are cleansed may fall from grace and depart from the living God." What can bring greater sorrow than to see one who has enjoyed the spirit of the Gospel and the power of the Holy Ghost fall from grace and turn to evil practices?  How careful we should be to walk the way of truth and constantly be seeking the companionship of the Holy Spirit that we be not led into temptation and fall." (CHMR 1:94)

In Nauvoo, Ill., the Prophet Joseph Smith said; "…according to the scripture, if men have received the good word of God, and tasted of the powers of the world to come, if they shall fall away, it is impossible to renew them again, seeing they have crucified the Son of God, afresh, and put Him to an open shame; so there is possibility of falling away; you could not be renewed again, and the power of Elijah cannot seal against this sin, for this a reserve made in the seals and power of the priesthood." (HC 6:252-253)

In the D&C 20:29-34, The Lord tells us, "And we know that all men must repent and believe on the name of Jesus Christ, and worship the Father in his name, and endure to the end, or they cannot be saved in the kingdom of God. And we know that justification through the grace of our Lord and Savior Jesus Christ is just and true; and we know also, that sanctification through the grace of our Lord and Savior Jesus Christ is just and true, to all those who love and serve God with all their might, minds, and strength. But there is a possibility that man may fall from grace and depart from the living God; Therefore, let the church take heed and pray always, lest they fall into temptation; Yea, and even **let those who are sanctified take heed also.**"

Alma 39:6 "For behold, if ye deny the Holy Ghost when it once has had a place in you, and ye know that ye deny it, behold, this is a sin which is unpardonable; yea, and whosoever murdereth against the light and the knowledge of God, it is not easy for him to obtain forgiveness; yea, I say unto you, my son, that it **is not easy for him to obtain a forgiveness.**"

# The following questions are by an unknown author:

"Whether we understand the theological definitions of the Gospel or not, here are some critical questions that we need to address relative to our salvation, and exaltation.

Have you received the ordinances of baptism and confirmation by one having authority in the Church of Jesus Christ of Latter-day Saints? Have you offered up an acceptable sacrifice of a broken heart and contrite spirit? Do you sustain the President and all the General Authorities of the Church as prophets, seers and revelators? Are you an active, faithful member of the Church who strives diligently to keep all the commandments and magnify your callings? Do you sustain your Bishop and priesthood leaders?

Do you pray always, feast daily on the words of Christ, and keep yourself unspotted from the world? Has the Lord revealed unto your mind and your heart with unmistakable certainty that you have received a complete forgiveness of all your sins and do you know with perfect assurance that you are holy, without spot; clean, pure and spotless every whit? Do you know with perfect assurance that you are saved, or redeemed, from the fall; that you have obtained salvation from all sin and have overcome the world? Do you know without doubt that your sacrifice is totally acceptable before Him? Have you received the endowment of charity in your life? Does the Lord confirm to your heart your righteous state and the promise of eternal life? Do you enjoy the constant companionship of the Holy Ghost? Have you received a mighty faith in Christ, which enables you to obtain revelations and perform miracles in His name?

If you can answer yes to all of these questions, through the revelation and confirmation of the spirit, then you are truly sanctified, or saved, and have the perfect assurance that, if you retain this blessed state to the end of your probation, you shall perfect your claim on your inheritance and receive the more sure word of prophesy making your calling and election to eternal life sure.

# Author's Note

I hope that you will continue your research on these sacred topics, and study the words of the past and the living prophets and apostles. This volume is only a small portion of the inspired words available on these subjects, to those who study it out for themselves.

It is my prayer that this book has inspired you to take the steps to sanctification, and to believe that it will happen for you, if you stay on the straight path. Believe Christ, and believe that with God all things are possible, even the purification of those who have greatly sinned, because the Lord loves the sinner not the sin. Your Heavenly Parents love you, perfectly and unconditionally, forever, because you are their child!!!. Their greatest joy is having you, one of their choice children, come home and inherit All that they have!!!

The Holy Spirit will help you, just ask and you will receive personal instructions, directions and encouragement in your quest to be spiritually born of God. The sacrifices will seem like pennies compared to the diamonds of spiritual gifts and blessings you will receive both in this life and in the world to come! Remember that "all things are possible to him that believeth."

May the Lord's choicest blessings always be poured upon you, as you strive to consecrate your life to Him, and as you always remember Him that you may always have His Spirit to be with you.

I say these things in the Holy name of our Savior, Jesus Christ. Amen.

# *Abbreviations*

AF "Articles of Faith" by James E. Talmage. Salt Lake City: Deseret Book Company, 1924.

CR "Conference Report" of general annual or semi-annual conference of the Church.

DGSM "Doctrines of the Gospel" (student manual, Church Educational System) Salt Lake City:

JD "Journal of Discourses" 26 vols. Liverpool: R.D. and S.W. Richards, 1854-56.

LDPDC "Latter-day Prophets and the Doctrine and Covenants" compiled by Roy Doxey, 4 vols. Salt Lake City: Deseret Book Company, 1978.

PCG "Priesthood and Church Government" by John A. Widtsoe, Salt Lake City: Deseret Book Company, 1939 (compiled under the direction of the Council of the Twelve Apostles and copyrighted by the Church.)

TLDP "Teachings of the Latter-day Prophets" Salt Lake City: The Church of Jesus Christ of Latter-day Saints, 1986.

TPJS "Teachings of the Prophet Joseph Smith "Compiled by Joseph Fielding Smith. Salt Lake City: Deseret Book Company, 1976 (the original was published by the Church, in 1938)

fn footnotes
sel. Selections
com. Compiled

# Bibliography

"Discourses of Wilford Woodruff" sel G. Homes Durham, Salt Lake City, Bookcraft, 1946.

"Doctrine and Covenants Commentary" by Hyrum M. Smith, and Janne Sjodahl Deseret Book, 1978

"Doctrines of Salvation" by Joseph Fielding Smith. 3 vols. Salt Lake City: Bookcraft, l954-56

"Exodus to Greatness" by Preston Nibley: Deseret News Press, l947

"Evidences and Reconciliations" Ed. by G. Homer Durham, Salt Lake City: Bookcraft, l960

"Faith Precedes the Miracle" by Spencer W. Kimball, Salt Lake City: Deseret Book Company, 1972

"Gospel Doctrine" by Joseph F. Smith, 5th ed, Salt Lake City: Deseret Book Company, 1939

"Gospel Ideals" by David O. McKay, Salt Lake City: Improvement Era, 1953

"Gospel Truth" sel. by Jerrald L. Newquist, 2 vols, Salt Lake City: Deseret Book Company, 1957

"Key to the Science of Theology" by Parley P. Pratt, 9th ed. Salt Lake City: Deseret Book Company, 1965

"Learning for the Eternities" by Marion G. Romney, compiled by George J. Romney, Salt Lake City, Deseret Book Company, 1977

"Look to God and Live" by Marion G. Romney, compiled by George J. Romney Salt Lake City: Deseret Book Company, 1971

"The Life of Heber C. Kimball" by Orson F.Whitney, Bookcraft, 1947

"The Millennial Messiah" by Bruce R. McConkie, Salt Lake City: Deseret Book Company, l982

"The Mortal Messiah" by Bruce R. McConkie, Salt Lake City: Deseret Book Company, 1979-81 4 Vols.

"The Miracle of Forgiveness" by Spencer W. Kimball, Salt Lake City: Bookcraft, l969

"Mormon Doctrine" by Bruce R. McConkie, 2nd ed. Salt Lake City: Bookcraft, 1966

"A New Witness for the Articles of Faith" by Bruce R. McConkie: Bookcraft, 1985

"Not Withstanding My Weakness" by Neal A. Maxwell: Deseret Book, l981

"On the Way to Immortality and Eternal Life" by J. Reuben Clark, Salt Lake City: Deseret Book Company, 1961

"Prayer" Salt Lake City: Deseret Book Company, 1977

"The Presidents of the Church" by Preston Nibley: Deseret Book, 1945

"The Promised Messiah" by Bruce R. McConkie, Salt Lake City: Deseret Book Company, 1978

"A Rational Theology" by John A Widtsoe, Salt Lake City: Deseret Book Company, 1915

"Stand Ye in Holy Places" by Harold B. Lee, Salt Lake City: Deseret Book Company, 1974

"Teachings of Ezra Taft Benson" ed. Salt Lake City: Bookcraft, 1988

"Teachings of Lorenzo Snow" ed. by Clyde J. Williams, Salt Lake City: Bookcraft, 1984

"The Vitality of Mormonism" by James E. Talmage, Boston: Richard G. Badger1919

"The Way to Perfection" by Joseph Fielding Smith, Salt Lake City: Genealogical Society of Utah, 1940

"Why the Religious Life?" by Mark E. Petersen, Salt Lake City: Deseret News Press, 1930

"A Witness and a Warning" by Erza Taft Benson: Deseret Book, 1988

# INDEX

# "Have You Spiritually Been Born of God?"

Chapter 5
Pres. Brigham Young, TLDP, p. 604
Pres. Brigham Young, JD 2:123, JD 9:288
Elder Mark E. Peterson, "Why the Religious Life?" p. 252-253
Elder Bruce R. McConkie, "The Mortal Messiah" 4:114
Elder Delbert L. Stapley, CR Oct 1966
Elder Orson Pratt, JD, 17:112, LDPDC Vol 3, p. 456-457

Chapter 6
Prophet Joseph Smith, TPJS p. 149-150
Elder Parley P. Pratt, "Key to Science of Theology" p. 61. DGSM p. 45
Pres. John Taylor, JD, May 18, 1862, 10:57. JD 23:374
Pres. Brigham Young, JD 4:22, JD 6:98
Elder George Q. Cannon, "Gospel Truth" 1:343-344
Elder John A. Widtsoe, TLDP 276-277
Elder Bruce R. McConkie, "The Millennial Messiah" p. 98-99
Elder Joseph Fielding Smith, "The Doctrines of Salvation" 1:39
Elder Orson F. Whitney, CR April 1930, p. 134-135, LDPDC 3:92
Elder James E. Talmage, "The Articles of Faith" p. 147
Pres. Brigham Young, JD 3:211
Elder James E. Talmage, AF 151-152

Chapter 7
Pres. Ezra Taft Benson, "A Witness and a Warning" p. 73-79
Elder Marion G. Romney, CR, Oct 1955, p. 124
Elder Parley P. Pratt, Hymn p. 180

Chapter 8
Elder George Q. Cannon, CR Oct. 1899, p.50
Pres. Ezra Taft Benson, "A Witness and a Warning" p. 61-62
Prophet Joseph Smith, "Evening and Morning Star" Aug. 1832, TPJS p. 12
Pres. Harold B. Lee, "Stand Ye in Holy Places" p. 60
Elder J. Reuben Clark, "On the Way to Immortality and Eternal Life" p. 5
Pres. Brigham Young, JD, Apr. 18, 1874, 17:40
Pres. Young relates the words Joseph Smith said to him in a dream.
"Exodus to Greatness" by Preston Nibley p. 329
Elder Bruce R. McConkie, "The Promised Messiah" p. 351

Chapter 9
Elder Bruce R. McConkie, "A New Witness for the Articles of Faith" p. 282, 288
Elder Bruce R. McConkie, "The Promised Messiah" p. 227, 349
Elder Neal A. Maxwell, "Not Withstanding my Weakness" p. 73

**Chapter 12** (continued)
Elder Marion G. Romney, CR, Oct 1945 p. 15-16
Pres. Brigham Young JD Dec. 18, 1853, 2:132
Pres. Joseph F. Smith, "Gospel Doctrine" p. 49-50
Pres. Joseph Fielding Smith, LDPDC 4:404
Pres. Gordon B. Hinckley, Boston Mass. Regional Conference, Apr. 22, 1995
First Presidency. MS, July 8, 1854, 16:429-430
Elder George F. Richards, CR, Oct 1944, p. 88
Prophet Joseph Smith, "Lectures on Faith" 7:9
Elder Bruce R. McConkie, "A New Witness for the Articles of Faith" p. 149
Elder Bruce R. McConkie, "The Mortal Messiah" 3:81, 130
Elder John A. Widtsoe, "Evidences and Reconciliations" p. 32

**The following list consists of inspiring books, which focus on being spiritually born of God.**

"Born of the Spirit" Richard Packham, Bookcraft, Salt Lake City, Ut. 1979

"Experiencing the Mighty Change" published in1998 call 801 825-4222

"Following the Light of Christ into His Presence" John M. Pontius, CFE, Springville, Ut. 1997

"I Need Thee Every Hour, the Joy of Coming to Christ" Blaine M. Yorgason, Deseret Book Company Salt Lake City, Ut. 2003

"Knowing Christ" George Pace, CFI Springville, Ut. 1996

"Spiritual Survival in the Last Days" Blaine M. Yorgason, Deseret Book Company, Salt Lake City, Ut. 1990

"Spiritual Progression in the Last Days" Blaine M. Yorgason, Deseret Book Company, Salt Lake City, Ut. 1994

"Spiritual Plateaus" Glenn L. Pace, Deseret Book Company, Salt Lake City, Ut. 1991

"The Mighty Change" Elaine Cannon & Ed J. Pinegar Deseret Book Company, Salt Lake City, Ut. 1992

www.haveyouspirituallybeenbornofgod.com